U.S. Education Reform and National Security

COUNCIL *on*
FOREIGN
RELATIONS

Independent Task Force Report No. 68

Joel I. Klein and
Condoleezza Rice, *Chairs*
Julia Levy, *Project Director*

U.S. Education Reform and National Security

The Council on Foreign Relations (CFR) is an independent, nonpartisan membership organization, think tank, and publisher dedicated to being a resource for its members, government officials, business executives, journalists, educators and students, civic and religious leaders, and other interested citizens in order to help them better understand the world and the foreign policy choices facing the United States and other countries. Founded in 1921, CFR carries out its mission by maintaining a diverse membership, with special programs to promote interest and develop expertise in the next generation of foreign policy leaders; convening meetings at its headquarters in New York and in Washington, DC, and other cities where senior government officials, members of Congress, global leaders, and prominent thinkers come together with CFR members to discuss and debate major international issues; supporting a Studies Program that fosters independent research, enabling CFR scholars to produce articles, reports, and books and hold roundtables that analyze foreign policy issues and make concrete policy recommendations; publishing *Foreign Affairs*, the preeminent journal on international affairs and U.S. foreign policy; sponsoring Independent Task Forces that produce reports with both findings and policy prescriptions on the most important foreign policy topics; and providing up-to-date information and analysis about world events and American foreign policy on its website, www.cfr.org.

The Council on Foreign Relations takes no institutional positions on policy issues and has no affiliation with the U.S. government. All views expressed in its publications and on its website are the sole responsibility of the author or authors.

The Council on Foreign Relations sponsors Independent Task Forces to assess issues of current and critical importance to U.S. foreign policy and provide policymakers with concrete judgments and recommendations. Diverse in backgrounds and perspectives, Task Force members aim to reach a meaningful consensus on policy through private and nonpartisan deliberations. Once launched, Task Forces are independent of CFR and solely responsible for the content of their reports. Task Force members are asked to join a consensus signifying that they endorse "the general policy thrust and judgments reached by the group, though not necessarily every finding and recommendation." Each Task Force member also has the option of putting forward an additional or dissenting view. Members' affiliations are listed for identification purposes only and do not imply institutional endorsement. Task Force observers participate in discussions, but are not asked to join the consensus.

For further information about CFR or this Task Force, please write to the Council on Foreign Relations, 58 East 68th Street, New York, NY 10065, or call the Communications office at 212.434.9888. Visit CFR's website at www.cfr.org.

Task Force Members

Task Force members are asked to join a consensus signifying that they endorse "the general policy thrust and judgments reached by the group, though not necessarily every finding and recommendation." They participate in the Task Force in their individual, not institutional, capacities.

Carole Artigiani*
Global Kids, Inc.

Craig R. Barrett
Intel Corporation

Richard Barth
KIPP Foundation

Edith L. Bartley
UNCF

Gaston Caperton
The College Board

Linda Darling-Hammond*
Stanford University

Jonah M. Edelman*
Stand for Children

Roland Fryer Jr.
Harvard University

Ann M. Fudge

Ellen V. Futter*
American Museum of Natural History

Preston M. Geren
Sid W. Richardson Foundation

Louis V. Gerstner Jr.

Allan E. Goodman
Institute of International Education

Frederick M. Hess
American Enterprise Institute for Public Policy Research

Shirley Ann Jackson*
Rensselaer Polytechnic Institute

Joel I. Klein
News Corporation

Wendy Kopp
Teach For America

*The individual has endorsed the report and signed an additional or dissenting view.

Contents

Foreword

It will come as no surprise to most readers that America's primary and secondary schools are widely seen as failing. High school graduation rates, while improving, are still far too low, and there are steep gaps in achievement between middle-class and poor students. Even in the midst of high unemployment rates, business owners are struggling to find graduates with sufficient skills in reading, math, and science to fill today's jobs. School districts, teachers' unions, and parents are engaged in fierce debates over the best way to rein in climbing costs and improve standards. Meanwhile, progress is frustratingly slow, if in fact what is taking place represents progress at all.

The domestic consequences of a weak education system are relatively well known. The Council on Foreign Relations (CFR) made the decision to sponsor this Task Force to address the less well known— yet equally sobering—national security repercussions. In 2011, CFR launched its Renewing America initiative, which examines domestic issues such as infrastructure, energy security, and the federal deficit that affect the United States' ability to conduct foreign policy and compete economically. Education is a critical component of this initiative. A world-class education system is vital to preserving not just the country's physical security but also to reinforcing the broader components of American leadership, such as economic dynamism, an informed and active democracy, and a coterie of informed professionals willing and able to live and serve around the world.

In international tests of literacy, math, and science, American students rank far below the world's leaders in Finland, South Korea, and Shanghai. They spend fewer years studying a more limited range of foreign languages than students in most other wealthy countries and just 1.4 percent of them study abroad, mostly in Europe. Significant majorities of young Americans are unable to identify strategically or politically important countries, such as Iraq or Afghanistan, on a map of the world; enrollment in civics and government classes is declining.

As a result, students are leaving school without the math and science skills needed for jobs in modern industry. They are too often unable to pass military entrance exams. The State Department and intelligence services lack sufficient linguists and analysts for critical regions. By almost every measure, U.S. schools are failing to provide the kind of education our society will need to ensure American leadership in the twenty-first century.

This Independent Task Force examines the critical weaknesses of the U.S. K-12 education system and assesses the actual and potential impact on American national security. While the system's present flaws, including a sclerotic bureaucracy, a lack of incentive for innovation, and few rewards for excellent teacher performance, are serious and their effects on students severe, the Task Force nonetheless sees cause for hope. The Common Core, a set of educational standards shared among all but five U.S. states, is due to be rolled out in 2014 and will set national expectations for student achievement in math and reading. President Barack Obama's Race to the Top program allowed states and school districts compete for a share of $5 billion to fund programs designed to improve student assessments, reward excellent teachers, and rapidly improve the worst-performing schools. These efforts build on President George W. Bush's No Child Left Behind Act, which was the first federal effort to measure and publicize student test results, and the success of charter schools and voucher programs, which allow families to choose the best school for their children. Clearly, change is possible, as is cooperation across party lines.

The Task Force recommends three overarching reforms to improve the educational system and enhance America's future ability to safeguard the country, compete and collaborate with others, and reinforce American leadership worldwide. First, it calls on governors to not only adopt the state-led Common Core curriculum, but also expand the curriculum to include skill sets—such as science, technology, and foreign languages—that are critical to national security. The Task Force also advocates structural changes that will empower students and their families to choose which schools they attend. Lastly, this report calls on state governors, working in conjunction with the federal government, to establish a national security readiness audit that holds educators and policymakers responsible for meeting national expectations in education.

It is important to emphasize, though, that this report is the beginning of a conversation, not the end of one. American teachers, administrators, policymakers, and parents all need to think about how to better prepare students for life in a world that will affect them, directly and indirectly, in countless ways. Young people will need not only the skills outlined here but also a deep and diverse knowledge base about the world around them. The histories and foreign policies of other countries, the nature and function of the international system, and an understanding of the challenges and opportunities globalization offers—these could all be elements of a curriculum dedicated to shaping the globally literate citizens our civil service, military forces, economy, and society writ large will need. As policymakers consider the important reforms proposed here, I hope they will do so with a mind toward these potential next steps.

I would like to thank the Task Force's distinguished chairs, Condoleezza Rice and Joel Klein, for their leadership and commitment to this endeavor. This Task Force brought together a collection of exceptional individuals, each with very different backgrounds and opinions, to reach a consensus on an issue that is often controversial and always incites great passion. I am grateful to all of the Task Force members and observers for contributing their time and informed perspectives to produce this report.

I also invite readers to review the additional views written by several Task Force members that appear at the report's conclusion. The report of an Independent Task Force is a document that represents the consensus among the group, and each signatory endorses the broad thrust of the policy recommendations. However, these additional views provide valuable insight into the breadth of the debate and demonstrate the complexity of the issues at hand.

My thanks also extend to Anya Schmemann, CFR's Task Force Program director, without whose guidance this project would not have been possible. I would also like to thank Project Director Julia Levy, who wove together the many perspectives represented by this Task Force in a report that we hope helps generate a national conversation.

Richard N. Haass
President
Council on Foreign Relations
March 2012

Chairs' Preface

Under its Renewing America initiative, the Council on Foreign Relations has focused attention on the domestic sources of American strength and global leadership. Education is one of those core strengths—and its erosion will undermine the United States' ability to lead.

When we as chairs convened this Task Force, we asked, Why is K-12 public school education a national security issue?

First, it is critical that children in the United States be prepared for futures in a globalized world. They must master essential reading, writing, math, and science skills, acquire foreign languages, learn about the world, and—importantly—understand America's core institutions and values in order to be engaged in the community and in the international system.

Second, the United States must produce enough citizens with critical skills to fill the ranks of the Foreign Service, the intelligence community, and the armed forces. For the United States to maintain its military and diplomatic leadership role, it needs highly qualified and capable men and women to conduct its foreign affairs.

Third, the state of America's education system has consequences for economic competitiveness and innovation. No country in the twenty-first century can be truly secure by military might alone. The dominant power of the twenty-first century will depend on human capital. The failure to produce that capital will undermine American security.

Finally, the United States cannot be two countries—one educated and one not, one employable and one not. Such a divide would undermine the country's cohesion and confidence and America's ability and willingness to lead. Opportunity and promise for all Americans are bedrock principles upon which this country was founded.

The United States is an exceptional nation in many ways. As a people, we are not held together by blood, nationality, ethnicity, or religion. The true American identity is born of the idea that it does not matter where you came from; it only matters where you are going. And thus, solutions to education must be unique and foster the American identity among citizens. The circumstance in which this American ideal is no longer obtainable for a substantial part of the American population is unacceptable.

While recognizing the improvement efforts already in progress, this report details the above concerns and offers recommendations to build upon the American education system today. This is a clarion call to the nation, aiming to magnify the need for change. We feel strongly that the United States must continue to provide an education that allows our country to lead the international community. The nation cannot allow Americans to lose confidence or the country to turn inward, resulting in a lack of American leadership around the world.

American education is vital to sustaining the nation's international leadership and competitiveness. And it is core to upholding the American ideals that our forefathers set out to establish in this democracy. We took on this project because we believe that the crucial question for our generation is whether the American Dream becomes the American memory on our watch. We believe and hope that the American Dream can still be sustained.

Joel I. Klein
Condoleezza Rice
Task Force Chairs

Acknowledgments

The report of the Independent Task Force on U.S. Education Reform and National Security is the product of a great deal of effort by the members and observers of the Task Force, and I am very appreciative of the time, attention, and expertise that each member devoted to this important project.

In particular, I would like to thank our distinguished chairs, Joel Klein and Condoleezza Rice, for their leadership, dedication, thoughtful direction, and constructive feedback on draft after draft. Joel and Condi come from different backgrounds and perspectives but are both inspirational in their passion for bringing people together to confront the challenges in U.S. education. It has been a true pleasure to work with both chairs and their teams, in particular Georgia Godfrey, Madeline Kerner, and Rosanne Mullaly.

It is striking how often politicians, executives, and other leaders in American life discuss the challenges America faces without addressing education—which is so intimately tied to long-term U.S. competitiveness, prosperity, and security. K-12 education reform is an unfamiliar topic for CFR, and I applaud the organization for having the vision and courage to take it on.

Throughout the process, I have been deeply appreciative of the Task Force members' and observers' time and attention and of their invaluable expertise and guidance. Many members took time to share detailed comments. Several, including Craig Barrett, Louis Gerstner, and Randi Weingarten, made presentations to the full group. I am also thankful to several people who met with and briefed the Task Force group, including U.S. secretary of education Arne Duncan, Mary Cullinane, formerly of Microsoft, Sir Michael Barber of Pearson, and David Coleman of Student Achievement Partners.

I also received help and support from CFR members. The New York Meetings team organized an event at the 2011 Term Member

Conference with CFR term members in New York, which I led with Task Force member Edith Bartley; and the New York Corporate Program organized an event for CFR corporate members in New York with Joel Klein and me.

I am grateful to many at CFR: The Publications team assisted in editing the report and readied it for publication. CFR's Communications, Corporate, External Affairs, and Outreach teams all worked to ensure that the report reaches the widest audience possible. Additionally, CFR's Events teams in both New York and Washington deserve thank yous for ably coordinating all of the Task Force's meetings.

Kristin Lewis, Shelby Leighton, and Elizabeth Leader of CFR's Task Force Program were extremely helpful and ensured the Task Force ran smoothly, from organizing meetings to researching and editing multiple drafts. Task Force Program director Anya Schmemann was instrumental to this project from beginning to end, offering invaluable advice and guidance.

I am grateful to CFR President Richard N. Haass for giving me the opportunity to direct this effort. I also would like to thank the Broad Foundation for its generous support of the project. CFR also expresses its thanks to the Bernard and Irene Schwartz Foundation for its support for the Renewing America initiative.

This report is the product of the Independent Task Force. I am convinced that its power is in its ability to reframe U.S. education reform and draw the attention of new leaders to the vital challenges this country faces. Throughout the writing and editing process, I have made every effort to take feedback and edits into account, but I take responsibility for the report's content and note that any omissions or mistakes are mine. Once again, my sincere gratitude to all who contributed to this effort.

Julia Levy
Project Director

Task Force Report

Introduction

Education has historically given all Americans—rich and poor, black and white—opportunity. It has allowed individuals to achieve their dreams, and it has fueled the continued innovation, growth, prosperity, and security of this nation. Today, however, as America's young citizens are simultaneously confronted with growing economic inequalities and an increasingly global and competitive world, elementary and secondary (K-12) schools are failing to provide the promised opportunity. Measured against global standards, far too many U.S. schools are failing to teach students the academic skills and knowledge they need to compete and succeed. Many are also neglecting to teach civics, the glue that holds our society together.

This failure and its consequences are not theoretical; they are real and already having a noticeable impact on individual students, particularly the neediest students for whom education is the only "intervention" capable of putting them on track to a better life, as well as on U.S. competitiveness, readiness, and future prospects. *In short, America's failure to educate is affecting its national security.* Consider the following points:

- *Despite sustained unemployment, employers are finding it difficult to hire Americans with necessary skills, and many expect this problem to intensify.* For example, 63 percent of life science and aerospace firms report shortages of qualified workers.[1] In the defense and aerospace industries, many executives fear this problem will accelerate in the coming decade as 60 percent of the existing workforce reaches retirement age.[2]

- *Most young people do not qualify for military service.* A recent study on military readiness found that 75 percent of U.S. citizens between the ages of seventeen and twenty-four are not qualified to join the military because they are physically unfit, have criminal records, or have inadequate levels of education.[3] The 25 percent of students who drop out of high school are unqualified to serve, as are the approximately 30 percent of high school graduates who *do* graduate but do not know enough math, science, and English to perform well on the mandatory Armed Services Vocational Aptitude Battery.[4]

– *The U.S. State Department and intelligence agencies are facing critical language shortfalls in areas of strategic interest.* Fewer than half of State Department officers in language-designated positions in Iraq and Afghanistan met the department's language requirements, for example, and shortfalls in strategically important languages such as Chinese, Dari, Korean, Russian, and Turkish are substantial.[5]

In many ways, the United States remains a global leader: its scholars win the most Nobel Prizes; its companies hold the most science and technology patents; and its armed services are, by many measures, the strongest in the world. However, no country in the twenty-first century can rest on its laurels or be truly secure by military might alone. Human capital will determine power in the current century, and the failure to produce that capital will undermine America's security.

TASK FORCE GOALS

As part of its ninetieth anniversary, in 2011 the Council on Foreign Relations began focusing on America's sources of domestic strength and leadership. Education is one of those core strengths, and it was clear to the Task Force from the beginning that its erosion would have a negative and sweeping impact on the country. Without mastery of core academic subjects, students are not prepared to collaborate, compete, or interact locally or globally. They are not prepared to create the innovations that drive economic growth or to fill critical positions in the Foreign Service, intelligence agencies, and the armed services. Educational failure puts the United States' future economic prosperity, global position, and physical safety at risk. Leaving large swaths of the population unprepared also threatens to divide Americans and undermine the country's cohesion, confidence, and ability to serve as a global leader.

CFR launched the Independent Task Force on U.S. Education Reform and National Security to draw attention to the problems in America's K-12 schools, which the group argues constitute a very grave national security threat facing this country. The Task Force members hope that by drawing attention to the undeniable—though often unconsidered—link between K-12 public education and national security, they will be able to recast old debates, spark new conversations, enlist new advocates, and catalyze national change. The group warns that mere tweaks to the status quo will not create the necessary transformation.

After elucidating the linkages between education and national security, exploring the current state of education in America and international comparisons, and identifying the core skills students need to learn, the Task Force proposes three overarching policy recommendations:

– *Implement educational expectations and assessments in subjects vital to protecting national security.* With the support of the federal government and industry partners, states should expand the Common Core State Standards, ensuring that students are mastering the skills and knowledge necessary to safeguard the country's national security. Science, technology, and foreign languages are essential—as are creative problem-solving skills and civic awareness. Across America, and especially in underserved communities, it is essential that necessary resources accompany these enhanced standards to fuel successful implementation.

– *Make structural changes to provide students with good choices.* States and districts should stop locking disadvantaged students into failing schools without any options; this is bad for the students and bad for the United States as a whole. Enhanced choice and competition, in an environment of equitable resource allocation, will fuel the innovation necessary to transform results.

– *Launch a "national security readiness audit" to hold schools and policymakers accountable for results and to raise public awareness.* There should be a coordinated, national effort to assess whether students are learning the skills and knowledge necessary to safeguard America's future security and prosperity. The results should be publicized to engage the American people in addressing problems and building on successes.

The Task Force believes that the United States' most foundational strengths are its liberty, democracy, capitalism, equality of opportunity, and unique ability to generate innovation. Without a wide base of educated and capable citizens, these strengths will fade, and the United

States will lose its leading standing in the world. Urgent shifts in education policy are necessary to help the country hold onto its status as an educational, economic, military, and diplomatic global leader.

The Education Crisis Is
a National Security Crisis

Why is education a national security issue? The Task Force members believe America's educational failures pose five distinct threats to national security: threats to economic growth and competitiveness, U.S. physical safety, intellectual property, U.S. global awareness, and U.S. unity and cohesion. The Task Force does not deny America's military might, but military might is no longer sufficient to guarantee security. Rather, national security today is closely linked with human capital, and the human capital of a nation is as strong or as weak as its public schools.

ECONOMIC PROSPERITY AND
INTERNATIONAL COMPETITIVENESS

The U.S. education system is not adequately preparing Americans to meet the demands of the global workforce.

When the U.S. government first measured educational attainment in 1947, only about half of Americans graduated from high school, compared to about 75 percent today.[6] In the mid-twentieth century, it was possible to build a meaningful career without completing high school. Today, this is not the case: the gaps in income and achievement between those with and those without college degrees are large and growing (see Figure 1), as are the educational opportunities available to the children of parents with and without education.[7]

Economists and employers predict that in the coming years, a growing number of U.S. citizens will face unemployment because of disparities between the workforce's education and skills and those needed by employers. Nobel Prize–winning economist Michael Spence recently explained that globalization is causing "growing disparities in income and employment across the U.S. economy, with highly educated workers enjoying more opportunities and workers with less education facing declining employment prospects and stagnant incomes."[8]

International competition and the globalization of labor markets and trade require much higher education and skills if Americans are to keep pace. Poorly educated and semi-skilled Americans cannot expect to effectively compete for jobs against fellow U.S. citizens or global peers, and are left unable to fully participate in and contribute to society. This is particularly true as educational attainment and skills advance rapidly in emerging nations.

A highly educated workforce increases economic productivity and growth. This growth is necessary to finance everything else that makes the United States a desired place to live and a model for other countries.

The opportunity of obtaining a top-rate education has historically attracted many immigrants to the United States from around the world. In turn, immigrant populations have contributed greatly to economic and social development in the United States. As a 2009 CFR-sponsored

FIGURE 1. MEDIAN ANNUAL EARNINGS (IN CONSTANT 2009 DOLLARS)

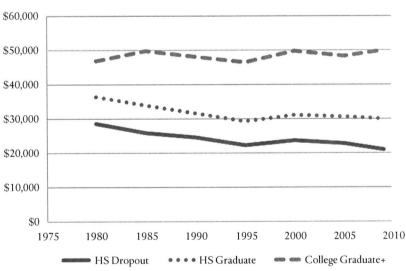

Source: "The Condition of Education: Learner Outcomes" (Washington, DC: National Center for Education Statistics, 2010), table A-17-1, http://nces.ed.gov/programs/coe/tables/table-er2-1.asp.

Independent Task Force report on U.S. Immigration Policy noted, "One of the central reasons the United States achieved and has been able to retain its position of global leadership is that it is constantly replenishing its pool of talent, not just with the ablest and hardest working from inside its borders, but with the best from around the world."

Too many schools have failed to provide young citizens with the tools they need to contribute to U.S. competitiveness. This, coupled with an immigration system in need of reform, poses real threats to the prospects of citizens, constrains the growth of the U.S. talent pool, and limits innovation and economic competitiveness.

THE COUNTRY'S PHYSICAL SAFETY

The U.S. educational system is not adequately preparing its citizens to protect America or its national interests.

To protect national security, the United States needs to maintain a robust military; yet currently, by the Department of Defense's measures, 75 percent of American young people are not qualified to join the armed services because of a failure to graduate from high school, physical obstacles (such as obesity), or criminal records.[9] Schools are not directly responsible for obesity and crime, but the lack of academic preparation is troubling: among recent high school graduates who *are* eligible to apply, 30 percent score too low on the Armed Services Vocational Aptitude Battery to be recruited.[10] The military aims to recruit high school graduates who score high on the aptitude battery because graduating from high school and performing well on the battery, which assesses students' verbal, math, science, and technical knowledge, predict whether recruits will succeed in the service.[11]

As with other measures of U.S. preparedness, there is a large racial achievement gap on the Armed Services Vocational Battery: one study found that African-American applicants are twice as likely to test ineligible on the battery as white applicants.[12] Similarly, 66 percent of applicants, including 86 percent of African-American applicants and 79 percent of Hispanic applicants, do not score well enough on the General Technical Exam to qualify for the U.S. Special Forces.[13]

U.S. schools are also failing to prepare enough scientists, mathematicians, and engineers to staff the military, intelligence agencies, and other government-run national security offices, as well as the aerospace and defense industries. Today, less than a third of American students graduate with a first university degree in any science or engineering field. More than half of these students have studied social or behavioral sciences; only 4.5 percent of U.S. college students, overall, graduate with degrees in engineering. In China, by comparison, more than half of college students receive their first university degree in science or engineering. Six percent study social and behavioral sciences, and 33 percent graduate with a degree in engineering.[14] At the graduate level in the United States, about one-third of science and engineering students are foreign nationals.[15] Foreign students earn 57 percent of engineering doctorates in the United States, 54 percent of computer science degrees, and 51 percent of physics doctoral degrees.[16] Only a minority of these students can obtain visas to remain in the United States after graduation. Fewer still are eligible for the U.S. security clearances needed to work in many defense-sector jobs.

These factors make it harder for defense-related employers, both governmental and private sector, to find qualified candidates, leaving jobs unfilled. The shortage of skilled human capital both inflates personnel costs and strains the military's ability to develop and deploy technologies that can deter sophisticated adversaries.

Educational deficiencies put defense and intelligence agencies under unnecessary pressure. Here are two real-world examples:

- Many U.S. generals caution that too many new enlistees cannot read training manuals for technologically sophisticated equipment. A former head of the Army's Training and Doctrine Command said that the lack of fully qualified young people was "an imminent and menacing threat to our national security."[17]
- An after-action report from a U.S. military intelligence headquarters in Iraq found that, of a staff of 250, only "four or five personnel were capable analysts with an aptitude to put pieces together to form a conclusion." The report continued, "In general, neither enlisted nor officer personnel were adequately trained to be effective analysts in a COIN (counterinsurgency) environment."[18] This deficiency means the national security community must pay more to attract qualified candidates or devote scarce resources to remedial training.

CLASSIFIED INFORMATION
AND INTELLECTUAL PROPERTY

Cyber espionage against government and business information systems is a troubling reality and an increasing threat.[19] The United States' adversaries are actively trying to infiltrate government and corporate networks to obtain valuable commercial and security data and information. The director of National Intelligence (DNI) reported recently that the volume of malicious software tripled between 2009 and early 2011.

In testimony before the House Committee on Energy and Commerce's subcommittee on oversight and investigations, then director of information security issues for the Government Accountability Office (GAO) Gregory Wilshusen said that criminals, hackers, disgruntled employees, hostile nations, and terrorists all pose real threats. He said, "the threats to information systems are evolving and growing, and systems supporting our nation's critical infrastructure are not sufficiently protected to consistently thwart the threats."[20]

The United States is arguably unprepared to mount a strong defense against this type of attack, partly because there are not enough people with the kind of technological expertise needed to do so. The chief information security officer at one of America's largest defense contracting firms told the Task Force in an interview, "The biggest challenge is the lack of qualified information security professionals. Without the right people, more technology will not do much good."[21]

U.S. GLOBAL AWARENESS

The lack of language skills and civic and global awareness among American citizens increasingly jeopardizes their ability to interact with local and global peers or participate meaningfully in business, diplomatic, and military situations.

The United States is not producing enough foreign-language speakers to staff important posts in the U.S. Foreign Service, the intelligence community, and American companies. A GAO report found that the State Department faces "foreign language shortfalls in areas of strategic interest."[22] In Afghanistan, the report found, thirty-three of forty-five officers in language-designated positions did not meet the State Department's language requirements. In Iraq, eight of fourteen officers did not have the necessary skills. Shortages in such languages as Dari, Korean, Russian, Turkish, Chinese languages, and others are substantial.[23] This leaves the United States crippled in its ability to communicate effectively with others in diplomatic, military, intelligence, and business contexts.

Too many Americans are also deficient in both global awareness and knowledge of their own country's history and values. An understanding of history, politics, culture, and traditions is important to citizenship and is essential for understanding America's allies and its adversaries.

A failure to learn about global cultures has serious consequences: a recent report by the U.S. Army Research Institute for the Behavioral and Social Sciences asserted that "cultural learning" and "cultural agility" are critical skills in the military.[24] What the authors call cross-cultural competence allows soldiers to correctly read and assess situations they encounter. It also gives them the tools they need to respond effectively and in line with the norms of the local culture. Finally, it helps them anticipate and respond to resistances or challenges that arise.

"Our forces must have the ability to effectively communicate with and understand the cultures of coalition forces, international partners, and local populations," U.S. secretary of defense Leon Panetta wrote in an August 2011 memo. "[The Department of Defense] has made progress in establishing a foundation for these capabilities, but we need to do more to meet current and future demands."[25]

THE UNITED STATES' SENSE OF UNITY AND COHESION

In a broader sense, the growing gap between the educated and the undereducated is creating a widening chasm that divides Americans and has the potential to tear at the fabric of society. As problems within the American education system have worsened, mobility that was possible in previous generations has waned. For the first time, most Americans think it is unlikely that today's youth will have a better life than their parents.[26] With wider income inequality and an increase in poverty, young people born to poor parents are now less likely to perform well in school and graduate from college than their better-off peers, and they are increasingly less likely to rise out of poverty.[27]

This trend not only causes the American Dream to appear out of reach to more citizens but also breeds isolationism and fear. The Task Force fears that this trend could cause the United States to turn inward and become less capable of being a stabilizing force in the world, which it has been since the mid-twentieth century.

In short, unequal educational opportunities and the resulting achievement gap have a direct impact on national security. Large, undereducated swaths of the population damage the ability of the United States to physically defend itself, protect its secure information, conduct diplomacy, and grow its economy. The unrelenting gap separating peers from peers also renders the American Dream off limits to many young people. Task Force members fear this inequality may have a long-term effect on U.S. culture and civil society.

The State of Education
in the United States Today

The Task Force believes that a strong K-12 education is not only critical for individuals to succeed in life, but also fundamental in determining whether the United States can defend itself, project its power, and thrive in a global economic environment.

Task Force members consider certain, specific skills essential to U.S. security and are adamant that all young citizens need a strong academic foundation in literacy and numeracy, as well as a sense of global awareness and a strong understanding of their nation's democratic values and practices. Thus, the Task Force worked to understand how well the K-12 system is preparing young Americans to be ready to help promote technological advancement, innovation, and economic, military, and diplomatic strength.

WHERE IS AMERICA IN TERMS
OF ACHIEVEMENT AND INVESTMENT?

The United States has many excellent elementary and secondary schools, but, on the whole, too many schools are falling short in achieving their basic objectives:

- They are not adequately preparing students for citizenship.
- They are not equipping the majority of students to effectively participate in an increasingly fast-paced and interdependent global society.
- They are not producing a sufficiently skilled military or workforce.

Too often, resources and expertise are not distributed equitably, leaving the students who face the greatest academic hurdles with fewer resources and more underprepared teachers and principals. Many American students—urban and suburban, rich and poor, black and white—suffer because of inadequate schooling, but the problems in American education are hurting minority and economically disadvantaged students the most. As a result, U.S. students have not been adequately competing with students in other developed countries.

The long-term trends in education are all the more disappointing because policymakers over the past three decades have been increasingly aware of the K-12 problems, have poured more and more resources into education, and have implemented scores of initiatives and programs intended to improve educational attainment. Selective improvements, innovations, and breakthrough transformations are not in question, but these advances have been overwhelmed by a "silver bullet" mentality of reform, a failure to follow through on implementation, and the ingrained and persistent weaknesses in U.S. elementary and secondary schools.

NECESSARY SKILLS FOR COMMUNITY AND INTERNATIONAL ENGAGEMENT

One of the earliest goals of the first public schools was to create an active and engaged citizenry. Too many U.S. public schools have stopped teaching civics and citizenship—leaving students without knowledge of their own national history, traditions, and values. Schools have also largely failed to help students become aware of other cultures or the world. This leaves students unprepared to exercise basic rights or fulfill core responsibilities.

In civics, about a quarter of American students are proficient or better on the National Assessment of Educational Progress (NAEP).[28] This leaves most twelfth graders unable to describe how laws are passed, unfamiliar with landmark Supreme Court decisions, and unsure of the functions of the U.S. Constitution or the Bill of Rights (Figure 2).[29]

Not only do American children know little about their own country, they also cannot understand or communicate with their global peers. Largely as a result of immigration, nearly four hundred languages are spoken within the United States.[30] However, roughly eight in ten Americans speak only English, and a decreasing number of schools are teaching foreign languages.[31] This failure to teach foreign languages (and a parallel failure to take advantage of the native language skills of immigrants) disadvantages Americans with respect to citizens of other countries, many of whom speak more than one language. For example,

*FIGURE 2. 2010 NAEP CIVICS PERFORMANCE OF FOURTH AND
EIGHTH GRADERS*

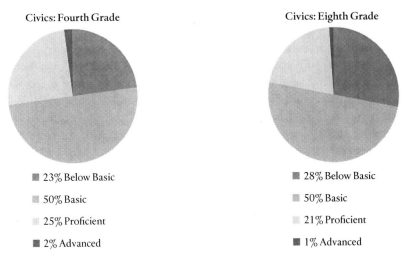

Civics: Fourth Grade   Civics: Eighth Grade

■ 23% Below Basic   ■ 28% Below Basic

■ 50% Basic   ■ 50% Basic

  25% Proficient   21% Proficient

■ 2% Advanced   ■ 1% Advanced

Source: "The Nation's Report Card: Civics 2010" (Washington, DC: National Center for Education Statistics, 2010), http://nces.ed.gov/nationsreportcard/pdf/main2010/2011466.pdf.

more than 35 percent of Canadians and 56 percent of Europeans speak more than one language.[32]

The Task Force does not necessarily believe that every U.S. student should be reading Chinese; indeed, too many are not reading English well enough. However, the group is troubled by the language deficit, and fears that it will prevent U.S. citizens from participating and competing meaningfully, whether in business or diplomatic situations. It will also have a negative impact on government agencies and corporations attempting to hire people knowledgeable about other countries or fluent in foreign languages.

READING, MATH, AND SCIENCE

Students who score "basic" on the NAEP have achieved only "partial mastery of prerequisite knowledge and skills." Students who score "proficient" have "demonstrated competency" over the knowledge and skills tested.[33] According to these nationally established cut points, about one-third of U.S. elementary and middle school students are demonstrating competency (or better) on national reading, math, and science exams (Figure 3).[34] This means that far too few students will be prepared to succeed in college or the workforce. Many students are growing up deficient in vital math skills, including knowledge of number properties and operations, measurement, geometry, data analysis, statistics, probability, and algebra.[35] They cannot recall, interpret, critique, or evaluate texts. They are unable to identify or use scientific principles in physical, life, or earth and space sciences, and they have failed to grasp science essentials such as the scientific method and inquiry-based learning.[36]

There have been some recent gains in math achievement at the elementary and middle school levels, but reading performance has been persistently flat. Despite recent advances, the average level of achievement among U.S. students has been problematically low for a long time, as demonstrated in Figure 4.

Low averages obscure deep and persistent resource and achievement gaps that separate poor students from rich students and black and Hispanic students from white and Asian students. These gaps have remained too wide, despite efforts and additional resources directed at helping students catch up.[37]

Gaps also separate U.S. states from one another, some routinely out-educating others. In almost any assessment of performance—math, reading, science, or the number of students graduating from high school on time—the map of the United States consistently shows the same pattern of over- and under-performance (Figure 5).[38] This means that students growing up in California or Nevada, for example, cannot expect the same quality of education as their counterparts in Massachusetts or Montana.

The differences in educational standards and opportunities across the United States put students who were simply born in the "wrong" neighborhood or state at a significant disadvantage, and leaves those states— and, by extension, the country—at a disadvantage.[39] The Task Force acknowledges concerns about the proper role of the federal government in K-12 education. The system garners considerable strength from the primary role of states and localities. But clearly there cannot be different standards and expectations for students or educators in today's world of labor and geographic mobility. The United States is a single country and every child here must have an equal chance at excellence.

Beyond the danger of creating massive disparity in educational attainment, these differences between districts and between states have another troubling effect: students who move frequently—such as the

FIGURE 3. STUDENT RESULTS IN READING, MATH, AND SCIENCE

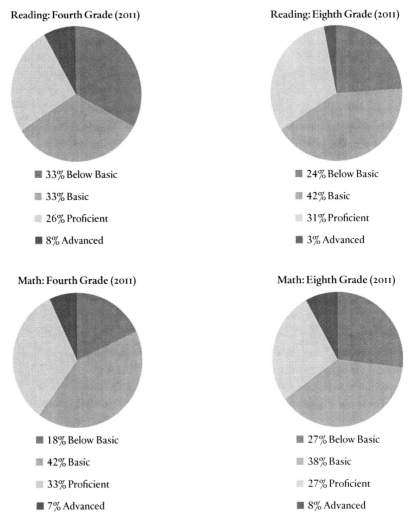

Reading: Fourth Grade (2011)

- 33% Below Basic
- 33% Basic
- 26% Proficient
- 8% Advanced

Reading: Eighth Grade (2011)

- 24% Below Basic
- 42% Basic
- 31% Proficient
- 3% Advanced

Math: Fourth Grade (2011)

- 18% Below Basic
- 42% Basic
- 33% Proficient
- 7% Advanced

Math: Eighth Grade (2011)

- 27% Below Basic
- 38% Basic
- 27% Proficient
- 8% Advanced

Source: "The Nation's Report Card," National Results, Achievement Levels, http://nationsreportcard.gov.

FIGURE 3. (continued)

Science: Fourth Grade (2009)

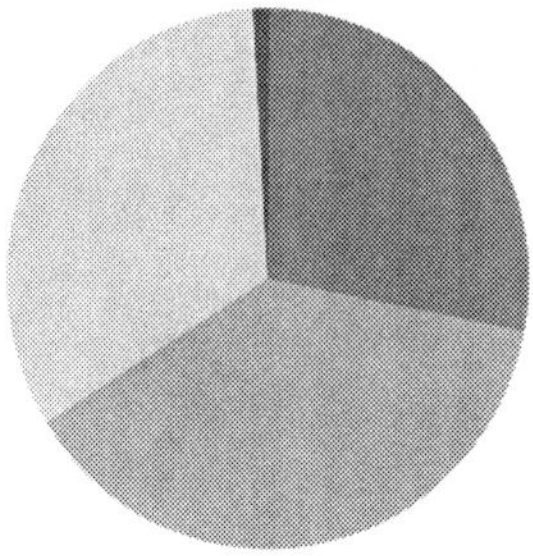

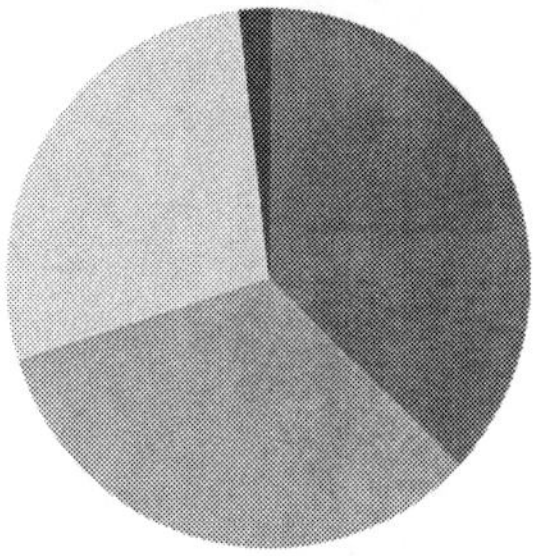

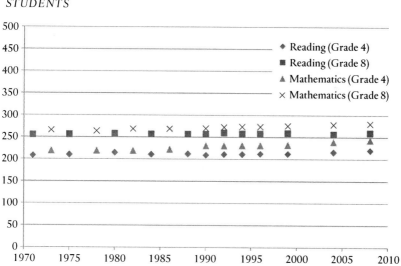

28% Below Basic
38% Basic
33% Proficient
1% Advanced

Science: Eighth Grade (2009)

37% Below Basic
33% Basic
28% Proficient
2% Advanced

FIGURE 4. TREND IN NAEP MATHEMATICS AND READING AVERAGE SCORES FOR NINE- AND THIRTEEN-YEAR-OLD STUDENTS

500
450
400
350
300
250
200
150
100
50
0
1970
1975
1980
1985
1990
1995
2000
2005
2010
Reading (Grade 4)
Reading (Grade 8)
Mathematics (Grade 4)
Mathematics (Grade 8)

Source: Bobby D. Rampey, Gloria S. Dion, and Patricia L. Donahue, "The Nation's Report Card: Trends in Academic Progress in Reading and Mathematics" (Washington, DC: National Assessment of Educational Progress, 2009), http://nces.ed.gov/nationsreportcard/pubs/main2008/2009479.asp.

FIGURE 5. FOURTH GRADE MATH NAEP 2009

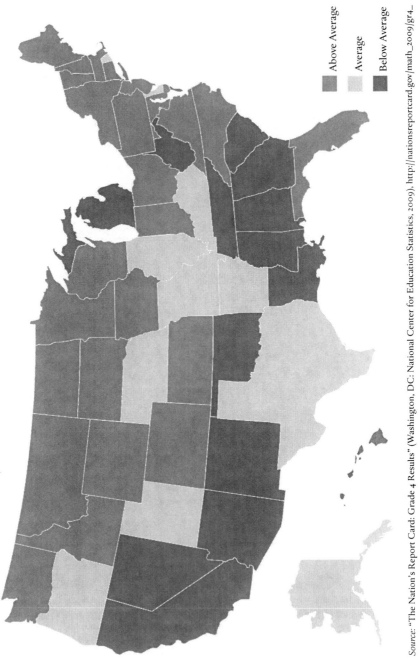

Above Average

Average

Below Average

Source: "The Nation's Report Card: Grade 4 Results" (Washington, DC: National Center for Education Statistics, 2009). http://nationsreportcard.gov/math_2009/gr4_state.asp?subtab_id=Tab_1&tab_id=tab1#tabsContainer.

more than one million children of military families—cannot expect to pick up at new schools where they left off.[40] This is a recruiting and retention problem for the armed services: the parents of school-age children will be hesitant to serve if their children's education will be at risk. This problem must be addressed.[41] It is worth noting that schools run by the Department of Defense outperform other schools, especially for minority students. However, these schools currently serve only 8 percent of the military-connected children in the United States.[42]

GRADUATION RATES

Not surprisingly, the challenges that students confront in the early grades persist when they enter high school: they are unprepared, they struggle in their courses, and they begin skipping school. This pattern often precedes dropping out of high school.[43] Nationwide, about 75 percent of U.S. students graduate from high school in four years.[44] As with results in core academic subjects, achievement gaps in the graduation rate are wide.[45] States' graduation standards—as well as states' success in graduating students—also vary widely (Figure 6).[46]

Evidence is mounting that K-12 schools are not adequately preparing students who *do* graduate from high school for college or work. Estimates of college readiness of U.S. high school graduates are disquieting. One recent report by the ACT, the not-for-profit testing organization, found that only 22 percent of tested high school students in the United States met "college-ready" standards in English, mathematics, reading, and science.[47] The same study found that only 3 percent of African-American students met these standards.[48] Even among those headed to college, only 43 percent met college-ready standards.[49] According to the Department of Education, 42 percent of students at two-year colleges and 39 percent of those at four-year colleges need to take remedial courses to attempt to relearn what they failed to master in high school.[50]

A lack of preparation in the K-12 system matters: colleges typically cannot make up for what students fail to learn at the secondary level. Evidence is increasing that students who require remedial classes in college tend to struggle and drop out. One government study found that students who enroll in a remedial reading course are more than 41 percent more likely than their counterparts to eventually drop out.[51]

FIGURE 6. STATES' PUBLIC HIGH SCHOOL GRADUATION RATES
(2008–2009)

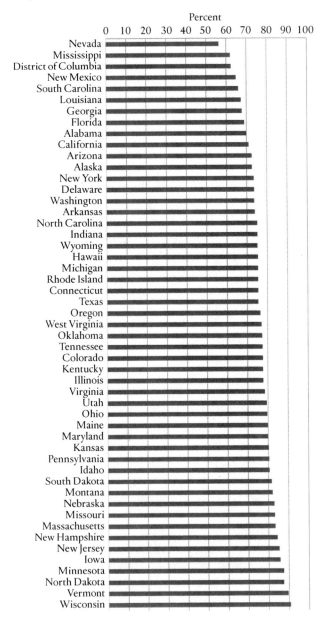

Source: Chris Chapman, Jennifer Laird, Nicole Ifill, and Angelina KewalRamani, "Trends in High School
Dropout and Completion Rates in the United States: 1972–2009," IES 2012-006 (Washington, DC:
National Center for Education Statistics, 2012), table 12, http://nces.ed.gov/pubs2012/2012006.pdf.

Failing to complete high school has a range of frightening consequences for students and society: dropouts are more likely to be unemployed, live in poverty, and end up in jail. They earn about $20,000 less annually than graduates.[52] Dropouts are about three times as likely to be unemployed as college graduates and three times as likely to live in poverty as those who enroll in college.[53] Nearly one in ten male high school dropouts is in jail or juvenile detention, compared with less than three in one hundred high school graduates and less than two in one thousand college graduates.[54] These statistics represent real people—millions of people who leave school each year with limited prospects and limited ability to contribute to society, and who too often become burdens to the country.[55]

U.S. PERFORMANCE VERSUS INTERNATIONAL PERFORMANCE

As the United States struggles to educate its youngest citizens, educational systems around the globe are steadily improving.

According to the results of the 2009 Program for International Student Assessment (PISA), an international assessment that measures the performance of fifteen-year-olds in reading, mathematics, and science every three years, U.S. students rank fourteenth in reading, twenty-fifth in math, and seventeenth in science among students in industrial countries.[56] The results of the test, administered by the Organization for Economic Cooperation and Development (OECD), show that since the exam was first administered in 1999, some European and Asian students have academically surpassed students in the United States.[57] For example, Germany, Luxembourg, and Hungary were behind the United States in math on the 2000 PISA exam. In 2009, however, each outperformed the United States.[58]

In 2009, when students in Shanghai, China, took the PISA for the first time, they outscored the average U.S. student in reading, math, and science.[59] This might not be an apples-to-apples comparison, but U.S. secretary of education Arne Duncan called the results "a wake-up call." He added, "I know skeptics will want to argue with the results, but we consider them to be accurate and reliable, and we have to see them as a challenge to get better. . . . We can quibble, or we can face the brutal truth that we're being out-educated."[60]

The results of international exams do not show merely that the average U.S. student is falling behind; they also show that the top students

FIGURE 7. 2009 PISA OECD COUNTRY RESULTS

Reading		Math		Science	
Country	Scale Score (2009 PISA)	Country	Scale Score (2009 PISA)	Country	Scale Score (2009 PISA)
Republic of Korea	539	Republic of Korea	546	Finland	554
Finland	536	Finland	541	Japan	539
Canada	524	Switzerland	534	Republic of Korea	538
New Zealand	521	Japan	529	New Zealand	532
Japan	520	Canada	527	Canada	529
Australia	515	Netherlands	526	Estonia	528
Netherlands	508	New Zealand	519	Australia	527
Belgium	506	Belgium	515	Netherlands	522
Norway	503	Australia	514	Germany	520
Switzerland	501	Germany	513	Switzerland	517
Estonia	501	Estonia	512	United Kingdom	514
Iceland	500	Iceland	507	Slovenia	512
Poland	500	Denmark	503	Poland	508
United States	500	Slovenia	501	Ireland	508
Germany	497	Norway	498	Belgium	507
Sweden	497	France	497	Hungary	503
France	496	Slovak Republic	497	United States	502
Ireland	496	Austria	496	Norway	500
Denmark	495	Poland	495	Czech Republic	500
United Kingdom	494	Sweden	494	Denmark	499
Hungary	494	Czech Republic	493	France	498
Portugal	489	United Kingdom	492	Iceland	496
Italy	486	Hungary	490	Sweden	495
Slovenia	483	Luxembourg	489	Austria	494
Greece	483	United States	487	Portugal	493
Spain	481	Ireland	487	Slovak Republic	490
Czech Republic	478	Portugal	487	Italy	489
Slovak Republic	477	Italy	483	Spain	488
Israel	474	Spain	483	Luxembourg	484
Luxembourg	472	Greece	466	Greece	470
Austria	470	Israel	447	Israel	455
Turkey	464	Turkey	445	Turkey	454
Chile	449	Chile	421	Chile	447
Mexico	425	Mexico	419	Mexico	416

Source: "Highlights from PISA 2009," NCES 2011-004 (Washington, DC: National Center for Education Statistics, 2010), http://nces.ed.gov/pubs2011/2011004.pdf.

in the United States would not be considered top students elsewhere in the world, particularly in mathematics. One recent report found that thirty countries have a higher percentage of advanced math students than the United States does. Only 6 percent of American students are advanced, against at least 20 percent in Taiwan, Hong Kong, Korea, and Finland.[61] Another study found that even the top-performing U.S. state, Massachusetts, is not at the top of the international pack in math.[62] Yet another found that students in wealthy U.S. public school districts would score in only about the fiftieth percentile in math relative to students in other developed nations. "If the city were Singapore," the report found, "the average student in Beverly Hills would only be at the thirty-fourth percentile in math performance."[63]

College attainment is another way to assess U.S. educational performance relative to other nations over time. This is relevant for an analysis of the K-12 system because success in college is an extension of prior academic success at the primary and secondary levels. For decades, about 40 percent of Americans have graduated from two- or four-year colleges. This level used to be the highest in the world, but is no longer.[64] The U.S. slippage in international rankings is best illustrated by examining college attainment by age cohort, as shown in the following series of charts.

In 2008, the percentage of Americans between the ages of fifty-five and sixty-four with a college degree was the largest percentage of any developed nation in that age cohort, according to the OECD (Figure 8). However, among those in the forty-five to fifty-four age cohort, the United States ranked third globally in 2008 (Figure 9).

For the youngest cohort measured, the international ranking is now tenth, as shown in Figure 10. These charts reflect the lack of progress in educational attainment in the United States as other countries are changing their practices and policies, making significant gains in the percentage of their citizens who graduate from college.

Some analysts blame the U.S. educational weakness on diversity, poverty, and governance. Although these factors may affect individual students or schools, an analysis from the OECD finds that they do not explain the poor U.S. international ranking. "The United States is not unique, at least not demographically or socio-economically," the report found.[65] It also held that many other countries have the same degree of diversity as the United States, but that socioeconomic disadvantages in the United States are more closely linked with poor academic performance than in other countries. Rates of childhood poverty are lower

FIGURE 8. COLLEGE ATTAINMENT OF AMERICANS AGES FIFTY-
FIVE TO SIXTY-FOUR

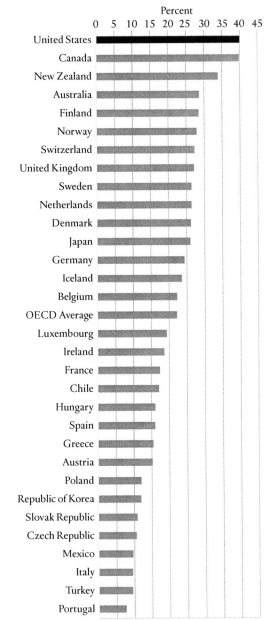

Source: Thomas D. Snyder and Sally A. Dillow, *Digest of Education Statistics, 2010*, NCES 2011-015 (Washington, DC: National Center for Education Statistics, 2011), table 421, http://nces.ed.gov/programs/digest/
d10/tables/dt10_421.asp.

FIGURE 9. COLLEGE ATTAINMENT OF AMERICANS AGES FORTY-FIVE TO FIFTY-FOUR

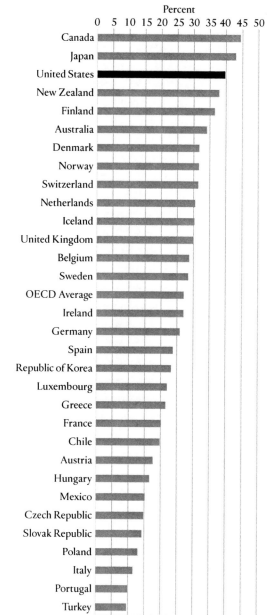

Source: Snyder and Dillow, Digest of Education Statistics, 2010.

FIGURE 10. COLLEGE ATTAINMENT OF AMERICANS AGES
TWENTY-FIVE TO THIRTY-FOUR

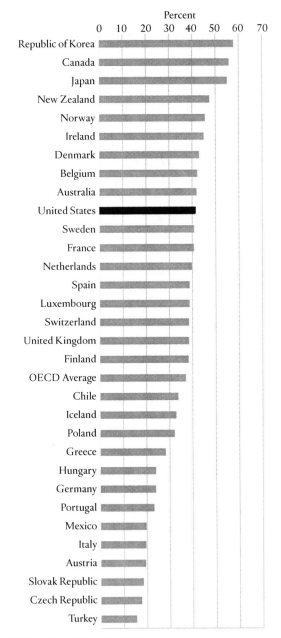

Source: Snyder and Dillow, Digest of Education Statistics, 2010.

in many high-achieving countries.[66] However, even privileged U.S. students are trailing in international comparisons in math achievement. For example, only 8 percent of white students and 10 percent of those whose parents went to college are advanced in math.[67] Overall, U.S. educational outcomes are unacceptably low. The United States has known for a generation that its K-12 system is slipping, but reform efforts have not made a major impact, and the United States is continuing to underprepare its young people. It is essential that all Americans—even those in relatively high-performing school districts—acknowledge this trend and take steps to address it.

INVESTMENTS IN EDUCATION

As student progress has stagnated, the United States has invested progressively more in education.[68] In the 1960–61 school year, per-pupil spending was less than $3,000 in 2008 dollars. In the 2007–2008 school year, per-pupil spending was $10,441, more than three times the earlier figure.[69] (These numbers do not include the costs of the dramatically mounting prices of pensions and other postretirement benefits for teachers and other staff members.)

This increased spending has fueled growth in the education bureaucracy, growth of school-level programs and practices, and growth in the teacher workforce. The number of teachers in the United States has more than tripled since the 1950s, cutting the student-teacher ratio nearly in half.[70] Some argue that the resulting class size reduction has benefited students, but many maintain that it has cost a great deal relative to its positive impact on student learning. Some of the additional spending on teachers is due to the growing costs of special education, but this does not explain all of the growth. According to the Department of Education, only about 20 percent of the teacher increase is due to the increase in special education teachers.[71]

The tripling in inflation-adjusted spending per student suggests a misallocation of resources and a lack of productivity-enhancing innovations. Per-pupil investment in education in other countries, including in some that are now outperforming the United States, is below the U.S. level. Finland's spending per student at the elementary level is about 30 percent less than that of the United States. Germany's is 40 percent less, Poland's 51 percent less. These trends are similar at the secondary level.[72]

Recent studies that have inspected the connection between investments in education and student outcomes have found that while U.S. schools are spending more overall, the big picture is complicated. There are large differences in the levels of funding allocated to schools. This means that the resources dedicated to educating a student are different from school to school, district to district, and state to state. Unlike some of its high-performing peers, the United States spends less to educate needy students than it does to educate well-off students. The United States also fails to track how efficiently and effectively it is employing its educational resources. One recent study found that "low productivity" in educational spending costs the United States $175 billion a year, 1 percent of the gross domestic product (GDP).[73] Further, the study found that unless there were new checks on the effectiveness of school spending, more spending would not necessarily improve student outcomes.[74] Given the magnitude of the challenge and past national investments at times of national security crises—from World War II to the terrorist attacks of September 11—increased spending on education may well be justifiable. However, more money alone is not the answer; education dollars must be spent wisely and efficiently, with real attention paid to eliminating waste and allocating scarce dollars to the work that has the largest impact on student learning. Resources are too often allocated to schools and students who will not benefit from them at the expense of students who desperately need them. Frequently, it also seems that resources are allocated without sufficient scrutiny over what dollars are buying. Thus, the Task Force calls for greater accountability and transparency in education budgets.

HOW ARE U.S. PUBLIC SCHOOLS ORGANIZED?

The existing systems and structures of education in the United States are laden with bureaucracy and inefficiencies. While there have been efforts to promote reform, many are too short-lived to engender widespread improvements, and successful innovations in one school too rarely spur change in other schools. Over the years, repeated efforts to improve the system have been constrained by the inflexibility of the system and by the expectations of adults, who, over the course of recent decades, have grown accustomed to the status quo.

STRUCTURE

U.S. elementary and secondary schools are not organized to promote competition, choice, and innovation—the factors that catalyze success in other U.S. sectors. Many institutions have overlapping authority over public elementary and secondary schools: the federal and all fifty state departments of education, more than thirteen thousand local school boards, and a smattering of big-city mayors. This tradition of decentralized control traces back to the Tenth Amendment, which declares that "the powers not delegated to the United States by the Constitution, nor prohibited by it to the States, are reserved to the States respectively or to the people."

Although certain laws and funding streams—such as those controlling special education, English language learners, and programs governing national accountability standards—emanate from Washington, most school governance is considered a state or local matter. In practice, three layers of government, as well as a range of nongovernmental influences such as unions, community groups, and parent organizations, play a role in almost everything that happens in each school.

"It is time to admit that public education operates like a planned economy," the legendary teachers' union leader Albert Shanker said in 1989. "It's a bureaucratic system where everybody's role is spelled out in advance, and there are few incentives for innovation and productivity. It's no surprise when a school system does not improve. It more resembles a Communist economy than our own market economy."[75]

The system has rampant inequities: schools in richer neighborhoods are often better funded than schools in poorer neighborhoods. A recent analysis of educational economics found that because schools that serve needier students struggle to attract high-paid, experienced teachers, "Inside nearly every urban school district in the country, teachers are paid more to teach middle- or upper-class students than to teach high-poverty students."[76] A recent OECD report found that though the United States is not unique in its population of poor or immigrant students, it is one of only three developed countries that invest less in high-needs schools than in well-off schools.[77]

The relative level and proportion of federal, state, and local dollars spent on education varies widely in a given school district, depending somewhat on local priorities, but mostly on local wealth, luck, and legacy. In Louisiana, for example, nearly 17 percent of education funds come from the federal government, versus only 4 percent in New Jersey.[78] But because the state and local governments of New Jersey invest more in education than those of Louisiana do, the per-pupil expenditure in New Jersey is nearly 60 percent more than that in Louisiana.[79]

The wide variation in spending does not stop at the state or district level. Within a district, individual schools can receive different levels of resources than other schools that serve similar student populations.[80] Not surprisingly, this variation in funding means that some schools can provide students with more services and better-paid, more experienced teachers than others.

LACK OF INNOVATION

Innovation is widely understood to be the engine that keeps America running—and the factor that has led to its success over the centuries.

In science, technology, retail, the arts, energy, and other sectors of the U.S. economy, it is easy to find examples of dynamic innovation: the light bulb, the Model T, Broadway musicals, Disney, jazz, the polio vaccine, Wal-Mart, the personal computer, the Internet, Starbucks, eBay, Netflix, Google, the Human Genome Project, the iPod, Facebook, and many others. Entrepreneurs around the world use and emulate these and other successful American models.

In education, it is hard to point to examples of successful and sweeping innovations that have changed the way schools are structured, the way teachers teach, and the way students learn. Given the innovation deficit in the public school system, it is perhaps not surprising that approximately 0.2 percent of U.S. K-12 educational spending is on research and development (R&D).[81] This is dramatically lower than that of the military or of virtually any private company. Overall, R&D spending constitutes 2.82 percent of the U.S. GDP.[82]

Of course, there have been some changes in recent years, but unfortunately the changes have not often had a dramatic impact on student outcomes. For example, by 2008, all public schools in the United States had at least one instructional computer with Internet access; the ratio of students to computers was about three to one. More than 90 percent also had projectors and digital cameras for instructional use, and more than 70 percent had interactive whiteboards.[83] It seems clear that technology has the power to help students learn in new ways, to assess more rigorously how much students are learning, and to help teachers tailor instruction to students' individual learning needs. But technology is largely still being used to advance old-style teaching and learning with old-fashioned uses of human capital. That is, computers and digital technology have thus far not been used innovatively to change the way the United States educates its students, but instead simply to reinforce past practices.

HUMAN CAPITAL

About 80 percent of resources in education fund human capital—teachers, principals, and administrators—but these resources are arguably not allocated as wisely as possible.[84] For example, educators are routinely treated uniformly, as if the most and the least effective are identical in value. In New York City, for example, a teacher with ten years of experience who has earned a master's degree earns $75,937 a year regardless of performance and regardless of whether he or she is teaching math, science, or physical education.[85] Though there are political debates about how to properly train and compensate teachers, it seems clear that the United States is failing to effectively attract, train, develop, and retain and adequately compensate educators. The reluctance to embrace new ideas in human capital management—such as teacher performance incentives—places high costs on the educational system, dampens innovation, and increases the turnover rate among the best educators. In the end, students are the biggest losers, but teachers suffer as well.

Teachers' and principals' importance is both intuitively obvious and proven by countless studies and reports.[86] Because educators can have such a profound impact, ensuring that students have the best possible teachers and principals should be a top priority. Unfortunately, evidence is abundant that the United States does not do enough to make sure that schools are stocked with top-notch educators. As a result, unqualified teachers are teaching too many students. Explanations for this troubling shortage of highly skilled educators are numerous:

- Education is not seen as a prestigious profession.[87] In surveys, college students say teaching is less prestigious, less of a challenge, and has fewer high-quality coworkers than other fields.
- The United States is recruiting most of its teachers from the bottom two-thirds of college classes, whereas top-performing countries are pulling from the top third.[88]

– Well-educated women have more career options today and are not as likely to go into teaching as they were in past decades.[89]

– The United States is not doing a good enough job of training new teachers for the job or professionally developing them once they are hired. Most states and districts also fail to provide teachers with any performance-based incentives.

– Most U.S. school districts grant tenure to teachers and principals after a few years with little attention to quality. Only a tiny proportion of new teachers are asked to leave in the first few "probationary" years.[90] Tenure exists in many other countries with higher-performing schools, but, coupled with the training and pipeline problems, poses real problems in the United States.

The U.S. approach to teacher talent differs from that of other countries with more success in attracting and retaining high-performing teachers. It sets the bar lower for people to enter the profession and then invests less in teachers, starting with their training and continuing throughout their careers. For example, in South Korea, teaching is seen as an important and honorable career: teachers are selected from the top 5 percent of students to be trained in competitive training universities, and their pay is similar to that of doctors and engineers (and they typically teach larger classes of students than American teachers).[91] In Finland, another high-performing country, teachers are paid similarly to U.S. teachers, but, as in South Korea, the selection and training process is rigorous.[92]

Trends exist in top-performing countries. According to the OECD, these countries have adopted the following important human capital strategies:[93]

– *Change the pipeline of people* coming into the profession by raising entrance standards to teacher training schools.

– *Improve the quality of teacher training* so that trainees master the subjects they will teach, spend more time in clinical settings, and learn how to quickly diagnose and address students' problems.

– *Improve teacher quality once teachers are in classrooms*, through mentorship and sharing of best practices and constant feedback from peers.

Given the clear significance of teachers on student outcomes, it is imperative that schools and districts seriously rethink the teacher pipeline, training, development, and practice. Teachers work in individual classrooms, but they collectively have a profound impact on the readiness and character of the next generation.

CURRENT POLICIES AND REFORM EFFORTS

NATIONAL POLICY

Concerns about poor educational performance have mounted in recent decades, leading to a series of high-profile reform efforts. In the late 1980s, President George H.W. Bush and Bill Clinton, then governor of Arkansas, held a National Education Summit, at which the fifty governors aimed to agree on national education goals. The group adopted targets that it planned to meet by the year 2000; the goals included increasing the high school graduation rate to 90 percent, improving the quality of teachers, and making U.S. students first place worldwide in math and science. Unfortunately, the policies needed to achieve these goals were never put into place.

Later, the Clinton administration enacted the Goals 2000: Educate America Act, which gave states support so that they could develop learning standards and help students achieve those standards. The George W. Bush administration subsequently worked with Democratic and Republican leaders in Congress to enact and implement No Child Left Behind (NCLB), which mandated stricter accountability and transparency in education. This marked the first time that states were required to measure student results and make them publicly available. When Congress did not agree to restructure and reauthorize NCLB, the Obama administration began granting NCLB waivers to states in exchange for their agreeing to education reform. The U.S. Department of Education emphasizes that to gain the flexibility the waivers provide, states must agree to raise standards, improve accountability, and make reforms to improve teacher effectiveness.

The Obama administration is seeking to shift the federal role so that the Department of Education does more to support innovation in states, districts, and communities, using competitive funding to motivate change. Some of the administration's main initiatives are Race to the Top, the Investing in Innovation Fund (i3), and School Improvement Grants. Race to the Top is a national competition in which a $4.35 billion pool of federal funds is allocated to select states that design and implement reforms to one or more of the following activities:

- adopting standards and assessments that prepare students for college and careers
- building data systems that measure student growth and success and inform teachers and principals about how to improve instruction
- recruiting, developing, rewarding, and retaining effective teachers and principals
- turning around the lowest-achieving schools

Race to the Top has pushed state and local education authorities to make some changes addressing accountability, choice, parent involvement, and more.

The federal government plays an important role in encouraging and rewarding positive change, but it is constrained in what it can do. In many cases, taking the brave steps required to transform the status quo is up to the states and individual school districts.

STATE-LED CHANGE EFFORT: THE COMMON CORE

For decades, each U.S. state and many cities set unique standards. The patchwork of learning standards and curricula is a prime example of the United States' failure to provide a strong, uniform K-12 education to all children.

Recently, state governors wisely recognized that U.S. high school graduates were unprepared for the academic demands of college, and that educators needed to prepare today's students to compete against people across the United States and around the globe. The governors, prodded by the "carrot" of increased funding provided by the Obama administration's Race to the Top initiative, collaborated to create the Common Core State Standards, a set of shared math and literacy standards—based on assessments of needed skills and knowledge—that have now been adopted by all but five states.[94] This extraordinary achievement is unprecedented in U.S. history. The standards are set to be rolled out in the 2014–2015 school year.

The Common Core is benchmarked to international standards and establishes a "staircase" of increasing complexity for elementary and secondary students. The hope is that, each year, students will build on what they have mastered in the previous year so that they graduate ready for college, careers, or military service. The Common Core is not a prescribed curriculum, but rather a set of shared expectations for what students will learn and be able to do. It teaches fewer concepts in each grade but promotes a deeper mastery of the included topics—those that evidence shows matter most in preparing for college and careers.

In literacy, the standards place a greater emphasis on students' ability to read, understand, and summarize informational texts than previous state standards. In recent history, U.S. elementary students have spent most of their time reading narrative fiction. The new standards aim to build knowledge from an early age by requiring that 50 percent of students' time between kindergarten and the fifth grade be spent reading informational texts. In addition, the standards place a greater emphasis on evidence-based writing. From the sixth grade onward, the standards will require students to analyze sources and develop conclusions in their essays, as opposed to writing only narratives or personal opinion essays. The new standards require that 80 percent of what high school students produce be written with the intent "to write to inform and to write to argue."

In mathematics, the standards replace an approach that has been wide but shallow. American students study more topics each year but master fewer mathematical concepts than their peers in high-performing countries. The Common Core, in contrast, gives teachers more time to teach, and gives students the ability to practice more and learn in a rigorous way.

A recent study that surveyed college instructors found that the Common Core standards are rigorous enough to give students the skills and knowledge they need to succeed in college-level math and English language arts (ELA) courses.[95] However, questions remain about how the states will implement the standards. Some estimates find that teachers will have to make major changes in their practices to meet the new standards. Costs are of course associated with training teachers and publishing new materials, and the initiative faces political challenges from those skeptical about educational consistency across states.

Nevertheless, if this initiative succeeds, it will be the first time in U.S. history that expectations for learning are commonly understood across the United States, and that all students in the country will have the hope of learning what they need to know to succeed in college and jobs on graduation from high school. It seems clear that in order for this effort to work, it is important to invest in implementation, not just in the standards themselves. The expectations for what students must learn under the new Common Core are different from today's curricula, and it will be important to help current educators learn how to align their practices with the new expectations.

OTHER IMPORTANT RECENT REFORM EFFORTS

In individual cities and districts across America, other education reform efforts have been numerous, and they have had varying levels of success. The following section highlights select prominent reform efforts:

Improving the Quality of Educators and Leadership

Many recent efforts have worked to mold strong educational leadership. Several states, along with some pioneering districts and universities, have created leadership development programs that have improved training and mentoring for school leaders and have demonstrated their ability to raise student achievement. In addition, many leadership development efforts have also been generated outside government. For example, the Broad Superintendents Academy works to train experienced leaders from business, education, military, government, and nonprofits to take charge of the United States' large school districts. New Leaders for New Schools seeks to train the next generation of principals.

Teach for America (TFA) sends thousands of the strongest graduates from America's top universities to teach in some of the United States' lowest-income communities for at least two years.[96] TFA's goal is to motivate its teachers to take up the causes of educational excellence and equity throughout their lives, from either inside or outside the system. TFA's ability to recruit more top college graduates than any other organization or business in the country is a cause for optimism.

Though these initiatives still represent only a small portion of all teachers and school leaders across the United States, they signal possibilities for how the system can tap and develop talent if it is more clearly focused on doing so in the future. The Task Force is encouraged that some of these leadership-focused reforms have helped create a new crop of educators and leaders who have taken charge of many classrooms and major school systems.

Prioritizing Accountability

Tracking results and holding schools accountable for student outcomes has been a central focus of education reform, particularly since the No

Child Left Behind Act became law in 2002. Despite significant progress in education accountability, a great deal of inconsistency remains in the quality of assessments and other metrics, and in what information is tracked, analyzed, and made publicly available. Some states, such as Florida, have implemented far-reaching policies to help parents understand how well their local schools are performing, but the usefulness of this effort is somewhat ambiguous because of questions about metric quality, and this level of transparency and public outreach is far from the national norm.

Consequences for failure are also inconsistent. Some districts and states ignore persistent school failure. Some seek to diagnose the problems and develop school improvement plans in response. Others have strict rules that force failing schools to restructure or shut down. Still others have what look like development plans or strict rules that are not applied uniformly. Recently, there has been evidence that restructuring failing high schools in New York City has helped engender positive change, but the policies that New York implemented are not yet in wide national use.[97] It seems clear that it is important to use information about which schools, programs, teachers, and principals are effective and which are not to inform decision-making and drive school improvement efforts.

Providing Better Choices to Families

In the past decade, school districts and community-based school reformers have tried to give parents the flexibility to choose the school best suited to their children. The idea is that this allows schools to innovate, introducing new ideas and new competitive forces into school systems and allowing families to consider the best fit for their children.

Public school choice has been available in some districts, such as Cambridge, Massachusetts, and San Francisco, California, for more than twenty years. Magnet schools have offered choices to families in many more cities since the 1970s. Charter schools are a relatively new addition to district choice options. Charters are public schools that receive public money but are not subject to some of the rules and statutes that apply to other public schools. In return for flexibility, charters are supposed to be held accountable for student performance. If they fail to meet expectations, they lose their charters and are forced to shut down. Traditional public schools, on the other hand, can typically continue operating indefinitely regardless of performance.

Some charter schools have better results than others, but the best-performing ones (which are typically in states with the best charter laws) show that disadvantaged students and those with high needs can learn in the right environments. Though research is ongoing, a comprehensive new study analyzing previous charter school research found that there is "ample evidence" that charter elementary schools outperform traditional public schools in both reading and math, and that charter middle schools tend to outperform in math.[98] Anther study found that the Knowledge is Power Program (KIPP) schools have a "very positive" influence on reading and math achievement. Researchers have shown that a KIPP school would move a student from the fiftieth percentile to the fifty-fourth percentile in reading and the fifty-ninth percentile in math in just one year.[99]

An encouraging large-scale example of the potential impact of charter schools is post-Katrina New Orleans. Though there is still a long way to go and some analysts disagree on the details, the city has made dramatic structural and leadership changes that have resulted in large performance gains: from 2006–2007, the school year after the storm, to 2009–2010, public schools in New Orleans gained an average of nearly twenty points on the state exams, versus a statewide average gain of 6.5 points.[100] Other districts have shown gains primarily by improving district-run schools that offer choices, including those with special governance arrangements, such as Boston's Pilot Schools. San Diego has embraced a decentralized model under which schools innovate and implement reforms and then share best practices. As a result, student performance on the NAEP Trial Urban District Assessment improved significantly in both of these cities between 2003 and 2009.

These examples counter the long-held view that being born without money or other advantages is an insurmountable obstacle to student success.

The Skills and Knowledge
Needed for Tomorrow

It is apparent to the Task Force that U.S. students are not developing
the knowledge and skills they need to contribute to America's future
economic growth or security.[101]

The federal government predicts the U.S. economy will add more
than 20.5 million jobs between 2010 and 2020, an increase of more
than 14.3 percent.[102] Most of the jobs will demand more than a high
school diploma. Based on Bureau of Labor statistics, a report by the
Georgetown University Center on Education and the Workforce found
that the U.S. economy would create 46.8 million new and "replacement"
jobs by 2018, 63 percent of which will require some college education.[103]

"The implications of this shift represent a sea of change in American
society," the Georgetown report warns. "Essentially, postsecondary
education or training has become the threshold requirement for access
to middle-class status and earnings in good times and bad. It is no longer
the preferred pathway to middle-class jobs—it is, increasingly, the only
pathway."[104] The report finds that the number of degrees conferred in
the United States each year would have to increase by 10 percent for
American schools to meet these new demands.[105]

MISMATCH BETWEEN TRAINING AND JOBS

The mismatch between the jobs that American students are preparing
for and jobs that are available or projected to grow is increasing. Not
surprisingly, a lack of education is a primary driver of the discrepancy.

One recent report estimated nearly 6 million more high school dropouts in 2020 than jobs available for dropouts. It predicted a shortfall of
up to 1.5 million workers with bachelor's degrees or higher in 2020. It
also found that students are failing to pursue studies that will prepare
them for the fastest-growing fields, including science, technology, engineering, and math.[106]

A report by the Business Roundtable reaches similar conclusions.[107] It found in a recent survey that more than 60 percent of U.S. employers are having difficulties finding qualified workers to fill vacancies at their companies.[108] Another survey found that 64 percent of companies are already struggling to hire qualified candidates with experience in management, science, and computer engineering.[109]

Still another recent survey found that more than half of the business leaders surveyed said they face a challenge in recruiting nonmanagerial employees with sufficient skills training and education, despite high unemployment. This need was magnified at smaller firms, nearly 70 percent of which reported having difficulty finding employees with the required skills.[110]

HIGH-DEMAND SKILLS

In recent decades, leaders in government, business, and beyond have come to agree that long-term investments in education are necessary to address the growing mismatch between education and skills. The Task Force agrees with this assessment. The question, then, is the specific areas that make sense for additional investment.

In surveys and interviews, most employers say the skills that are in high demand today are the same skills that students were supposed to be learning in school fifty or one hundred years ago: the ability to write and speak clearly and persuasively, the ability to solve problems and think critically, and the ability to work both independently and on teams. The difference today is that more skilled workers are needed than in the past.

In the past decade, a range of education and business groups have established frameworks for what students need to learn today; these frameworks tend to be broad and combine a mix of "old-fashioned" skills and knowledge, such as numeracy and literacy, with "twenty-first-century" skills, such as using digital tools to research and solve problems.

The Partnership for 21st Century Skills, for example, has called for focus in six areas:[111]

– the traditional core academic subjects
– twenty-first-century content, including global, financial, and environmental awareness

- learning and thinking skills, including creativity, critical thinking, problem solving, communication, and collaboration
- information and communications technology skills
- life and career skills, including time management, group work, and leadership
- twenty-first-century assessments that accurately measure the other five skills

Other frameworks are similar, but sometimes place additional emphasis on different skills, such as specific technology capabilities or the ability to work autonomously.[112] The Task Force believes that the existing frameworks serve an important purpose in highlighting the importance of education in preparing young people to take on important challenges, but it worries that some of the frameworks are too broad and vague and leave room for some critical skills and knowledge necessary to protect U.S. security from slipping through the cracks.

Recommendations

The failure of U.S. K-12 schools to prepare young Americans with essential skills and knowledge puts this nation's economic growth and competitiveness, physical security, information security, and national character at risk. Companies are left struggling to find talent within the United States and are forced to search outside this country's borders, the military is left without trained technicians, the State Department is left without diplomats fluent in essential languages, and persistent achievement gaps are placing the American Dream out of reach for millions of Americans.

Government, business, and community leaders should take immediate action to address this threat. Disregarding the crisis, delaying action, or ignoring the mounting negative impact that the state of schools is having on U.S. national security would exacerbate the existing problems and further jeopardize the United States' standing in the world and its future prospects as a global leader.

The Task Force members agreed that the group's prescriptions should build on America's democratic values, inherent capabilities, and experiences. Policy recommendations should respect the tradition of local control in education, but must also recognize the importance of high expectations and consistency of skills and knowledge across the country.

The Task Force sets forth three central recommendations:

- *Implement educational expectations in subjects vital to protecting national security.* The states should expand the Common Core State Standards, ensuring that students are learning the skills and knowledge necessary to safeguard the country's national security. Science, technology, and foreign languages are essential—as are creative problem-solving skills and civic awareness. It is essential that necessary resources accompany these enhanced standards to fuel successful implementation.

— *Make structural changes to provide students with good choices.* States and districts should stop locking disadvantaged students into failing schools without any options; this is bad for the students and bad for the United States as a whole. Enhanced choice and competition, in an environment of equitable resource allocation, will fuel the innovation necessary to transform results.

— *Launch a "national security readiness audit" to hold schools and policymakers accountable for results and to raise public awareness.* At the heart of this recommendation is the creation of more meaningful assessments and simulations of student learning and, then, a coordinated, national effort to create targets and repercussions tied to the Common Core. A high-publicity public awareness campaign linked to the audit will engage the American people.

IMPLEMENT MEANINGFUL EDUCATIONAL EXPECTATIONS IN SUBJECTS VITAL TO PROTECTING NATIONAL SECURITY

The Task Force believes that the United States needs to build a stronger foundation of skills and knowledge among its citizens. Without high quality standards, assessments, and accountability, citizens' life prospects are limited, and the United States' economic, military, and diplomatic security is severely impaired.

BUILD ON THE COMMON CORE

Because states are the leading operators of U.S. education policy, state governments—the governors, legislators, and their appointees—hold the key to America's national security. As state governors have demonstrated in recent years, they are in a position to lead.

The Task Force commends the governors who have come together to create Common Core State Standards for literacy and math, and it urges them to

— continue collaborating with each other, as well as with educators and leaders from industry, the military, and beyond, to reach consensus on a broader Common Core and an associated set of skills and knowledge that are essential to maintaining national security;

- develop an assessment strategy to ensure that student achievement is measured effectively; and
- develop an implementation and investment strategy to ensure that the standards are put in place.

ESSENTIAL SKILLS FOR NATIONAL SECURITY

Science Expectations

A seminal 1944 report to President Roosevelt, *Science, the Endless Frontier*, called on the United States to invest in science education and peacetime research and development to bolster and strengthen the nation. Today, the importance of science education to American national security is the same or even greater than it was in the 1940s.

The Task Force endorses the efforts of more than twenty states that are currently working to create ambitious, internationally benchmarked expectations in science, and urges the rest of the states to collaborate in the effort. Young people should start learning core scientific principles and methods in kindergarten so that, by the time they graduate from high school, they are able to understand and apply scientific principles.

Technology Expectations

Working with computers is not a skill of the future. Like science, it is decidedly a skill of today, which is fundamental to protecting U.S. physical security and secrets as well as to allowing U.S. businesses to innovate and grow.

Therefore, the Task Force urges governors to work with each other, as well as with educators and leaders in business and national security, to create shared, high expectations for the technology principles and skills that students should master, starting in the earliest grades. The Task Force recommends that technology expectations be thoroughly integrated with math, literacy, science, and foreign language curricula so that students learn how they might effectively apply technological skills in diverse and constantly evolving settings. Students should graduate from high school with technological dexterity; able to understand and work with hardware, software, and networks; and able to use technology to find and process information, fuel creation and creativity, and collaborate and communicate with others.

Foreign Language Expectations

Americans' failure to learn strategic languages, coupled with a lack of formal instruction about the history and cultures of the rest of the world, limits U.S. citizens' global awareness, cross-cultural competence, and ability to assess situations and respond appropriately in an increasingly interconnected world.

The Task Force does not argue that *all* U.S. children should begin studying strategic languages and cultures. However, the opportunity to learn these languages and about the people who speak them should be available to many students across the United States, and *all students* should have access to high-quality foreign language programs starting in the earliest grades. If all Americans grew up proficient in at least one language in addition to English, and if instruction about other countries' histories and culture were built into the standard K-12 curriculum, young people would develop better understandings of world cultures and be better equipped to converse, collaborate, and compete with peers worldwide.

Therefore, the Task Force urges governors to collectively create expectations for language learning and world culture and history, which would boost the next generation's cross-cultural competence and practical ability to communicate.

Thinking Creatively Beyond the Core

The 9/11 Commission highlighted four U.S. shortcomings that opened the door to the terrorist attacks. One of these was a failure of imagination on the part of U.S. security agencies.[113] In 2001, the failure to spot and connect the dots was catastrophic for the United States. The Task Force believes that all young people—those who aim to work in national security and those who aim to work in corporations or not-for-profit organizations—must develop their imaginations from an early age. This is increasingly important as information becomes more and more abundant and as the world becomes more interconnected and complex.

The United States has traditionally led the world in patent applications, inventions, and innovation. The Task Force members believe that to retain this important competitive edge, lessons in creativity—whether in the arts or in creative analysis or imaginative problem solving, must begin in early elementary school. These vital skills should be incorporated into extracurricular programs as well as woven into lessons of math, literacy, language, science, and technology and tested through interdisciplinary simulations.

The same goes for civics. As detailed in this report, students in the United States are not currently learning the basic rights and responsibilities of citizenship, which is leaving them both globally unaware and oblivious to the opportunities they have as U.S. citizens. The Task Force believes that this fundamental knowledge set should be integrated into students' formal and informal instruction, starting in the earliest days of their educations.

MEANINGFUL ASSESSMENTS

The Task Force commends the two consortia—the Partnership for Assessment of Readiness for College and Careers (PARCC) and the SMARTER Balanced Assessment Consortium (SBAC)—that are working to develop assessments that are aligned to the new state standards.

However, the Task Force cautions test- and policymakers to ensure that new exams are both aligned with the new Core standards *and* more meaningful measures of student learning. It is not enough to test the new standards in old ways. It is essential that newly adopted assessments require students to demonstrate that they have grasped material and can apply it in the future. The Task Force strongly urges the adoption of more technologically advanced assessments that simulate real-world applications of skills and knowledge. Current assessment formats fall short and have unfortunate, unintended consequences on teaching and learning. While elements of current testing models, such as multiple choice and short essay exams, might still have a limited place, the United States should look both inward and outward at classic and emerging testing models that show real promise and then aggressively implement assessments that more appropriately track student outcomes.

FOCUS ON IMPLEMENTATION

The Task Force is aware that ensuring that effectively preparing students will take more than simply establishing high expectations; effectively implementing the plan is equally important, and implementation requires substantial commitments of both effort and resources. State and district leaders should work to ensure that the schools that serve the neediest students receive their fair share of funding and their fair share of excellent teachers and school leaders who are capable of implementing the expanded Common Core to its full potential in the classroom. Changing the way resources are allocated is, of course, much easier to write than to do—but the Task Force does not see it as optional. Dollars and human capital must be allocated consciously and wisely in order to ensure that all students have access to the high quality, expanded Common Core that the Task Force is urging. The Task Force believes that though revamping expectations for students should be a state-led effort, a broader coalition—including the defense community, businesses leaders, the U.S. Department of Education, and others—also has a meaningful role to play in monitoring and supporting implementation and creating incentives to motivate states to adopt high expectations. To ensure smooth implementation of the expanded Common Core, the Task Force urges:

- The standards must be accompanied by different kinds of accountability systems, which use information to guide policy and practice, as well as more advanced assessments, mentioned above, which test essential skills like decision-making and problem solving. Better accountability and assessment systems will spur implementation by educators who are seeking professional success for themselves and academic success for their students.

- Because standards cannot teach themselves, governors, working with state and local education officials, must take steps to prepare current and future educators for the challenge. The U.S. Department of Education should create incentives to motivate governors and other state and local leaders to help existing teachers and principals prepare for, adopt, and implement the upgraded expectations for student learning. The U.S. Department of Education, working in conjunction with state, local, and higher education officials, should entice new teachers and principals into the profession with the expertise and skills necessary to effectively teach the new standards. To make this possible, universities should raise entrance standards and requirements for teacher training programs and districts should focus on educators' effectiveness from the moment they are hired and throughout their careers.

- Standards should not be seen as permanent. They should be routinely evaluated and improved to ensure that the standards are ambitious and functional. The Defense Policy Board, which advises the secretary of defense, and other leaders from the public and private sectors should evaluate the learning standards of education in America and periodically assess whether what and how students are learning is sufficiently rigorous to protect the country's national security interests. Changing the status quo and ensuring that America's schools do not slip further behind is not a task for trained educators alone; it is a shared responsibility and must be elevated to the highest levels.

Although it is important that most states agree if higher expectations are to affect most U.S. students, governors should not be deterred if they are initially unable to reach agreement. If only 10 or 15 percent of states initially concur on expectations and exams, they should proceed with implementation. Other states will catch up later, following the example of the first movers. This said, the Task Force strongly encourages the states with large numbers of military families to implement the new expectations soon so that the children of service members, who must move every two years as their parents relocate to new bases, can have as consistent an educational experience as possible.[114]

MAKE STRUCTURAL CHANGES THAT EMPOWER EDUCATORS, FAMILIES, AND STUDENTS TO CHOOSE

Public education is an essential institution in America's quest to provide equality of opportunity and to ensure that social and economic mobility are available to all children, regardless of circumstances. It is not hyperbole to say that a robust system of public schools is essential to U.S. democracy. The country's history—even its recent history— provides inspiring stories of people who came from humble circumstances, attended public schools, and are now at the very top of the economic ladder and in leadership positions in all sectors of society.

Today the United States faces even greater pressures on social mobility, particularly from globalization and the technological revolution, which reward high skill levels and brutally punish those who fall behind. The worrying trend toward growing socioeconomic inequality, noted throughout this report, has many causes. But one of the few interventions that the United States has and has always used to ensure social mobility is education. U.S. public schools thus shoulder, fairly or unfairly, even more responsibility for the country's well-being today than in the past.

To address the need for intervention in the lives of today's children, the Task Force supports giving parents a wider range of educational options and encouraging states and school districts to foster the school-level innovation that will lead to good options for families. Choice is especially important for poor parents, who are more likely to live in districts with underperforming schools. Within the public arena, mobility within a district (i.e., allowing children and families to select their schools), magnet schools, and charter schools can provide alternative educational opportunities for individual students. And as schools recognize that they must educate children effectively or lose students, they will be motivated to perform better. Coupled with necessary resources, well-prepared educators, and strong curricula, this motivation has the power to improve the quality of education.

Admittedly, it is too early to determine the full effect of school choice in systemic reform—but competition has a salutary effect in almost every other aspect of American life, including the United States' well-regarded higher education system, and K-12 public schools should arguably be no different.

Most, but not all, members of the Task Force believe that choice should be extended to private K-12 alternatives. Obviously, the ideal situation is one in which every neighborhood's school could provide high-quality education to all students, but this is not the world in which we live today. In reality, the United States already has a system in which parents can opt out of public education for their children. But because opting out is only possible for those with financial means, poor children are often trapped in failing schools. This is the worst form of inequality. Programs like the DC Opportunity Scholarships and other voucher programs help to level the playing field in this regard and ought to be encouraged as the United States works toward the day when the public education system can fully provide a quality education for all students.

School choice often leads to harsh debates. The Task Force has decided not to recommend a single, "correct" way for all districts to create new options and offer choice to parents and students. However, the group strongly urges each state, working in conjunction with its local school districts, to (without delay) prompt a conversation about school choice and adopt and implement a strategy that provides local families with the choices they need and deserve. There are many examples, some encouraging and some cautionary, from America and beyond that officials should look to when formulating their own choice plans. Strategies that officials should consider include:

– implementing public school choice programs, such as those in Boston, New York, and San Francisco

– redesigning or creating new traditional public schools and magnet schools, providing additional access to high-quality options

– offering vouchers, such as the DC Opportunity Scholarships, to students

– authorizing the creation of more high-quality charters, pilot schools, and other nontraditional-model schools that provide families with access to schools with distinctive approaches to teaching and learning (It is worth noting that in some districts, about five times as many families are applying to charters and other schools of choice than there are seats available. Policymakers should consider local demand when formulating their district's school choice plans.)

– creating structural changes and collective bargaining reforms that require all schools serving public school students to agree to school-based leadership agreements under which school leaders would agree to help students learn and achieve at high levels in exchange for receiving substantial discretion over hiring, how to use resources, how to attract students, and how to live up to learning expectations for students

As officials formulate their choice programs, it is essential that they simultaneously ensure that they are appropriately measuring schools' quality so families can access information about schools and make informed decisions. They must also be attentive to resource allocation and ensure that funds are allocated wisely and equitably. If schools are severely resource-constrained, they will not be able to innovate their way to success, and students will inadvertently be harmed. Schools supported with public funds must support all students, irrespective of race, national origin, religion, language, background, or disability. Finally, it is essential that states and school districts remain vigilant: if any school is failing to live up to expectations and is not serving students well, education leaders must intervene to make sure that families not only have options—they have good options.

LAUNCH NATIONAL SECURITY READINESS AUDIT TO LINK ACCOUNTABILITY TO NEW EXPECTATIONS AND RAISE PUBLIC AWARENESS

In order to catalyze reform and innovation and better safeguard America's national security, it is essential to measure how well students, teachers, and schools are measuring up. It is also clear that simply measuring results is not enough to ensure progress: accountability must also engender consequences and public awareness.

THE AUDIT

The Task Force recommends that the U.S. Department of Education create incentives to motivate states to work together to create an annual audit, which would help policymakers and citizens assess the United States' level of educational readiness. Accountability is not new to education, of course, but the expanded Common Core and the associated assessments urged in the Task Force's first recommendation will create new opportunities for meaningful, apples-to-apples comparisons between states and individual schools in participating states.

For the audit, states would collect school-level information on factors important to national security, including (subgroup disaggregated) answers to the following questions:

- How many students are passing their (expanded) Common Core courses?
- How well are students performing on end-of-year summative assessments?
- How many students are mastering important "national security" skills, such as learning foreign languages and computer programming?

- Are students graduating from high school within four years (or
  within five or more years)?
- What percentage of students are "college-ready"? Career-ready?
- What are the characteristics of each school? For example, what is a
  school's budget and average per pupil allocation? How many teachers
  are there? What is a school's attendance rate?

The audit should combine this state-reported data into a single report
that tracks educational outcomes nationally, by subgroup, and by state.
It should also compare U.S. performance to other countries. Some of
the skills measured in this audit are basic and do not seem directly tied
to national security. This is intentional; students must master reading,
math, and science because they are building blocks for everything else.

In addition to the subgroups tracked through NCLB (race/ethnicity,
limited English, special education, free and reduced-price lunch), the
Task Force recommends that the audit should have an annual section
assessing the condition of education of the one million school-age children who have one or both parents serving in the active duty forces, the
national guard, or the reserves. These children have unique needs, often
moving from school to school as their parents transfer to bases around
the country. Since military-connected children are more likely to enlist
when they grow up and since their parents are more likely to end their
service if their children's education is at risk, it is critical to monitor their
performance and ensure that educators are taking steps to address their
special needs. This is not simply a matter of ensuring that these students'
educational needs are adequately addressed; it is also a matter of making
sure that America's armed forces can continue to attract to and retain in
the service parents who care about their children's educational welfare.

It is important to emphasize that the Task Force is advising the collection and release of school-level data. While teacher and student data
are essential to developing instructional plans and school policies, the
Task Force does not advocate the public release of individual teachers'
or students' performance or names.

USE AUDIT TO SPUR ACTION

The collected information will catalyze two types of action:

- *Learning (proof of success or failure could help educators, students,
  parents, and others learn, adjust practices, and improve).* Teachers and

principals should use the results to highlight what is working and to learn from mistakes, and the most effective schools should share their techniques to help others emulate their success.

— *Consequences (proof of underperformance could spur interventions for teachers or schools).* Data about individual schools and the system as a whole should be used to evaluate what is working and what is not. Such analyses should catalyze changes in policies, from resource allocation to professional development for educators. Where schools are underperforming, districts and states should take responsibility for analyzing why and intervening. This could mean reallocating resources, recruiting stronger school leaders, helping schools redesign programs, or restructuring schools to create better options for students. When a charter school fails to meet the expectations delineated in its charter, there should be an intervention to ensure that it stops underperforming. This principle should be applied broadly to all K-12 public schools to ensure that the system is built around the best interests of students and national security.

The Task Force urges policymakers to stop allowing failing schools to persist in shortchanging more students. If a school is failing to live up to its commitments, policymakers should take the necessary actions to protect students from continued neglect.

USE AUDIT TO INFORM THE PUBLIC

The Task Force believes the annual audit should be aggressively publicized to help all members of society understand educational challenges and opportunities facing the country. This public awareness campaign should be managed by a coalition of government, business, and military leaders. It should aim to keep everyone in the country focused on the national goal of improving education to safeguard America's security today and in the future.

Astute use of media and communications have a proven ability to effect changes in mindsets and actions, and the group believes that a targeted, annual campaign, led by the Department of Education in collaboration with the U.S. states, the Departments of Defense and State, and the intelligence agencies, could have this impact. The Task Force hopes that this annual campaign will prompt serious and purposeful national dialogues and a new commitment to implementing meaningful change.

Conclusion

Three decades ago, in August 1981, President Reagan's secretary of education, T. H. Bell, gathered a panel of educators and business leaders to investigate the secretary's concern about "the widespread public perception that something is seriously remiss in our educational system."[115] In April 1983, the group detailed the problems in U.S. education in *A Nation at Risk*. The report warned of "a rising tide of mediocrity that threatens our very future as a nation and a people."[116]

The report was published about three decades ago, but the risks the report highlighted are much the same as those that this Task Force is describing today.

In 2012, the sad fact is that the rising tide of mediocrity is not something that belongs in history books. Despite selective improvement, the big picture performance of America's educational system is all too similar to results from three decades ago. Too many students are falling behind academically and are leaving high school unprepared for college and work. And though educational attainment has not changed significantly, demands on the workforce have increased, making success less attainable for many Americans. As a result, people in communities across the United States are increasingly being left behind.

Meanwhile, other countries are improving educational outcomes, making it harder and harder for Americans to compete. This is true both for young people who are new to the job market and for older Americans. Looking forward, semieducated and semiskilled citizens are likely to feel increasingly burdened, and they will be less able to contribute to and enjoy improving national standards of living.

A GROWING CONSENSUS FOR CHANGE

Nevertheless, although the big picture looks the same as it did decades ago, it would be a mistake to ignore the areas of progress in the American system since the 1980s. In the past decade, a number of efforts to transform school leadership, teaching, curriculum, accountability, choice, and technology have been successful. They have produced changes and improvements in individual schools. To date, such improvements have been selective and insufficient to lift the educational performance of whole districts or whole states. Nonetheless, they show what is possible in American education as a whole.

This is a critical moment of opportunity when the nation could finally implement the necessary changes in its school system to safeguard the country's national security in the coming decades. The basis for advancing dramatic reforms is growing:

– *Acknowledgment.* Public acknowledgment that educational attainment and performance is inadequate and that substantial reform is needed is gaining widespread acceptance. This is not a one-party issue or a geographically isolated need.

– *Leadership.* Increasing numbers of motivated, high-quality leaders are involved at all levels of education—from the classroom up to the national leaders in Washington—and are able to lead change efforts.

– *Successful models.* Hundreds of schools across the country have modified and reformed their educational processes and approaches to teaching and learning in ways that have helped students exceed standards and expectations. These experiences provide guidance into how to lift educational standards and performance for all students, including high-needs students.

– *Economic environment.* Today's environment of scarcity could actually help jump-start necessary reforms by highlighting the urgency of the problem. Rather than continuing to invest in the status quo, some administrators have instead chosen to invest in the programs and services that show the most promise.

– *Political environment.* Over the course of the past decade, support for meaningful educational reform has generally been bipartisan. Recent legislation—from No Child Left Behind to Race to the Top—has created a base for improved accountability and incentives, and gives hope that collaboration could lead to real advancements. Cross-sector support for school reform—from corporations, libraries, museums, and other organizations—is also growing.

These variables are important, and make this a time like no other to change the way the United States educates its children—and to achieve transformational reforms on a level never before achieved in the U.S. school system.

RESTORING AMERICA'S LEADERSHIP

The Task Force believes that, taken together, the outlined recommendations can reshape education in the United States and put this country on track to be an educational, economic, military, and diplomatic global leader.

By nearly every measure, the United States is falling short of its collective expectations in K-12 public education—leaving individual Americans, communities, and the nation vulnerable. For all Americans who care about the country's future, these results are of grave concern.

The United States will not be able to keep pace—much less lead—globally unless it moves to fix the problems it has allowed to fester for too long.

The Task Force believes that this country has a real but time-limited opportunity to make changes that would maintain the United States' position in the world and its security at home. Whether and how the nation acts at this moment depends on its collective answer to two questions: What kind of country is the United States? What kind of country does the United States want to be?

The Task Force hopes that the United States, as a whole, shares its answers to these questions and is willing to reevaluate the status quo and adopt necessary changes.

The Task Force is hopeful that consideration of America's education failings as a national security threat will mobilize new constituents, energize advocates, spur policymakers into action, and attract increased investments in reform efforts. This said, calling the crisis in education a national security concern is not a gimmick or an empty phrase: with a failing economy, a stalemated political system, and a waning international presence, the United States stands at a crossroads.

Americans can either accept U.S. decline or can come together to support and implement fundamental and radical changes that put the country back on track to fulfilling its promise and potential.

Additional and Dissenting Views

It was a privilege to join members of the Task Force in considering strategies for addressing the challenges faced by U.S. K-12 public schools in the twenty-first century. While I remain concerned about key elements of the report, I appreciate the openness of the chairs, project director, and members to comments, suggestions, and criticisms that many of us offered throughout the process. In my view, the report has been strengthened by these contributions. I hope that the entire effort will spark enlightened debate about ways this nation can support the neighborhood public school—the bedrock of communities—and also meet the needs of students, educators, and their schools as they prepare young people for fulfilling lives, productive work, and active citizenship in an interconnected, global society.

National security requires a healthy economy, energy independence, investments in research and development, strong defense, a thriving civil society, a respected and involved diplomatic corps, and, most of all, a healthy and high-functioning political system. (The current political environment is a clear demonstration of what happens when we have a public—and public officials—who are uninformed and/or ill-informed about our nation's history, our political system, and the values upon which it was built.)

Certainly schools must play a critical role in assuring that these needs of national security can be met. Yet, while some of the data are disturbing, nothing in this report convinces me that that our public schools "constitute a very grave national security threat facing this country." Indeed, claims of alarm can only set the stage for dramatic actions unsupported by evidence: in this case, market-based approaches to school reform, that, overall, have not demonstrated their effectiveness. Indeed, charter schools and vouchers are diverting funds and energy away from neighborhood schools, and the more successful ones rely on additional support from private sources ("voluntary taxation"), a situation that is neither sustainable nor scalable. Moreover, the drive toward "competition" can diminish individual commitment to the common good, thus undermining the very nature and purpose of public education: preparing young people of all backgrounds to become informed and active citizens who understand their rights and responsibilities to contribute to society and participate in the shaping of policies that affect their communities and the larger world.

I applaud the Task Force report's call for more attention to U.S. and world history and cultures, civics, science, and foreign languages. However, the well-intentioned emphasis on testing basic math and reading has diverted funding and attention from other areas of equal value. The proposed national audit will only increase the pressure to focus on standardized tests when funds to pay for this initiative could be better used if made available to the neediest school districts for classroom instruction.

Our public schools need flexibility and sufficient resources to identify and nurture young people's talents, interests, and imaginations, whether in the sciences, mathematics, technology, or the liberal and applied arts. Early and ongoing exposure to all of these subjects develops critical thinking and creative problem-solving skills, all essential to building a sound and sustainable economy—and also a society enriched and emboldened to take on the challenges before us in the twenty-first century.

My heartfelt thanks to the Council on Foreign Relations for the opportunity to participate in the Task Force.

Carole Artigiani
joined by Linda Darling-Hammond, Stephen M. Walt,
and Randi Weingarten

There is much to applaud in this report of the Task Force. I am pleased that the Task Force identifies the importance of setting high goals for student learning in fields ranging from English language arts and mathematics to science, technology, engineering, and foreign languages— areas that were profoundly neglected during the No Child Left Behind era. The report wisely calls for a richer and more internationally comparable curriculum for all children, beginning in elementary school, along with strategic investments that address the dramatic inequalities in funding that currently exist. This is critically important for our success as a nation, for the talent needed must be cultivated from all communities, among all our young people.

The report recognizes that new standards will not teach themselves, and that we must invest in the knowledge and skills of educators, especially those that serve our neediest students, from their entry into training and throughout their careers. In addition, the report has forcefully outlined the need for more innovative and authentic assessments of learning that evaluate critical thinking and communication skills, the ability to apply knowledge to real world problems, and the ability to find, analyze, and evaluate complex information in order to learn new things at all times. Both the ongoing high-quality training of professionals and the use of performance-based assessments are long-standing traditions of excellence in the armed services that could and should inform the ways we consider building systems in public education.

It is with respect to the features of strong systems that I raise specific concerns with the recommendations of the report. Although the report suggests, appropriately, that we must now compete with high-achieving nations around the world, its recommendations do not acknowledge the lessons these nations have to offer or the lessons we should learn from reforms in the United States.

One shortcoming is that this report accepts, uncritically and despite significant evidence to the contrary, that competition and privatization are essential—indeed perhaps the most important—strategies for improving public educational systems. It ignores the fact that the nations that have steeply improved achievement and equity and now rank at the top on the PISA tests (i.e., Finland, Singapore, and South Korea) have invested in strong public education systems that serve virtually all students, while nations that have aggressively pursued privatization, such as Chile, have a huge and growing divide between rich and poor that has led to dangerous levels of social unrest.

It also ignores research that raises serious cautions about the outcomes of unbridled privatization in education. Although I agree that many charters have done excellent work in serving diverse student populations, and I have personally worked closely with some of these schools, it is also true that the nation's largest multistate study on charter schools found that charters have been, overall, more likely to underperform than to outperform district-run public schools serving similar students. In addition, studies have found that, as a sector, charters serve significantly fewer special education students and English learners, and too many have found ways to keep out and push out students who struggle to learn. While touting the privatization of schools in New Orleans, the report fails to note that many high-need students have been rejected from charters there, that school exclusion rates are extraordinarily high, and that the Southern Poverty Law Center had to sue on behalf of special education students who were unable to gain admission to public schools. Meanwhile, New Orleans remains the lowest-ranked district in the low-performing state of Louisiana. Similarly, the report neglects to mention the many studies that have failed to find positive outcomes of voucher systems when similar students are compared. Finally, the report ignores the fact that our highest-achieving states have all built high-quality systems without charters, vouchers, educational management companies, or other forms of privatization.

To its credit, the Task Force acknowledges that there are many routes to high-quality choices in education, including options such as district magnet schools and other schools of choice within school systems; that choice must be accompanied by a level playing field in terms of resources; and that schools of choice should accept and support students irrespective of race, national origin, religion, language background, or disability. This is a start in the right direction, but if our goal is better education for all students and a stronger national capacity to educate all children, these matters deserve more serious deliberation. The path forward should be focused on building capacity to ensure high-quality options in all schools within a robust public education sector, as all high-achieving nations have done.

The report should also take a more evidence-based approach to the critical matter of developing a strong teacher workforce. While appropriately underscoring the need to invest in teaching, the report ignores many successful models of teacher preparation and development that have been shown to boost teacher effectiveness and retention. It holds up Teach for America (TFA) as the solitary model for entering teaching—despite the fact that recruits have only a few weeks of training when they enter and most leave their positions after two years, provoking churn and high replacement costs in the vulnerable schools they leave. While the commitment of TFA recruits is commendable, we need solutions like those developed at Columbia, Stanford, and many other top universities that recruit high-ability entrants and prepare them exceedingly well for long-term careers and leadership in education.

To do this, we will need to emulate nations like Finland and Singapore, which invest in recruiting top people and preparing them well—completely at government expense and with a stipend while they train—and often expect a minimum term of service (usually between three and five years) in exchange. Initial preparation and later professional development are intensive, high quality, and classroom relevant. Salaries are competitive with other professions, and administrators are well trained, so they can help teachers become more effective while keeping them in the profession.

As this report eloquently points out, we need to get serious about building a uniformly successful public education system in the United States, and this means we must learn from our own experiences and those of successful nations that we see as peers and competitors. Building systems requires a keen focus on what matters and what works, along with the discipline to not be distracted by silver bullets that cannot ultimately solve the pressing problems we face.

Linda Darling-Hammond
joined by Carole Artigiani, Stephen M. Walt, and Randi Weingarten

The great strength of this report is that it properly highlights the critical and too often ignored nexus between education and national security. It also correctly stresses the importance not only of reading and mathematics, but of science, foreign language and area studies, history, and social studies, and consistently focuses on student performance and teacher excellence.

While I question a few of the solutions prescribed and their precise application, the overarching value of the report is in establishing the vital link between high-quality, equally distributed education for our children and the security, prosperity, and overall well-being of our country and democracy.

Ellen V. Futter
joined by Jonah M. Edelman and Shirley Ann Jackson

Education is a public good, and I am therefore concerned about a complete privatization of education. While useful in many instances, vouchers and charter schools are not, in and of themselves, a systemic and systematic way to improve the quality of overall K-12 education in the United States.

I fully support the report's recommendation of full implementation and expansion of the Common Core State Standards to raise educational quality and to enhance coherence in our approach to public education in the United States.

Lastly, I believe that the approach of the Task Force report toward closing the gaps in achievement between disadvantaged children and their more affluent counterparts is not strong enough in its recommendations and does not address the multiple complexities involved in making change.

Shirley Ann Jackson

I am pleased to support the Task Force's effort to draw attention to the issue of public education. The report contains valuable information and some useful suggestions for reform, but in my judgment falls short in several areas.

First, the report exaggerates the national security rationale for reforming U.S. K-12 education. It says a troubled public education system is a "very grave national security threat facing this country," but it offers only anecdotal evidence to support this unconvincing claim. The United States spends more on national security than the next twenty nations combined, has an array of powerful allies around the world, and remains the world leader in science and technology. It also ranks in the top 10 percent of the world's 193 countries in educational performance, and none of the states whose children outperform U.S. students is a potential rival. Barring major foreign policy blunders unrelated to K-12 education, no country is likely to match U.S. military power or overall technological supremacy for decades. There are good reasons to improve K-12 education, but an imminent threat to our national security is not high among them.

Second, there is a mismatch between the report's alarmist tone and its core recommendations. In particular, if the current state of K-12 education were really a very grave threat to national security, the Task Force should emphatically support allocating greater resources to meet the challenge. Yet even though key recommendations, such as raising teacher quality, cannot be realized without additional public investment, the report offers only a bland statement that "increased spending may well be justifiable." It then declares that "money alone is not the answer," creating the unfortunate impression that the Task Force is trying to solve an alleged national security threat on the cheap.

Third, the call for a "national security readiness audit" of educational performance repackages the current focus on standards under a misleading label. The proposed audit would not measure "national security readiness," and it is not clear who will pay for these new reporting requirements or what the consequences of poor performance would be.

Fourth, there is no consensus among professional educators, academic scholars, or engaged citizens about the net impact of charter schools, vouchers, or other forms of privatization, because empirical evidence is mixed. The report leans heavily toward one side in this contested set of issues, however, thereby encouraging a policy course that could do more harm than good.

Finally, the report correctly emphasizes that improved teacher quality may be the single most important factor that would improve student achievement. Yet it offers few concrete steps for addressing this issue. Creating a serious national program of training and credentialing would not be cheap, but it could do more to improve our schools than simply providing greater "choice" or subsidizing various forms of privatization with public monies.

Education is vital for America's future, and the CFR Task Force deserves credit for tackling the issue head-on. But the report is best seen as one element of a larger conversation, and not as a reliable blueprint for reform.

Stephen M. Walt
joined by Carole Artigiani, Linda Darling-Hammond,
and Randi Weingarten

I was honored to participate in this Task Force. My hope was and is that its work would advance the crucial goal of strengthening America's public schools, which have been and must remain a fundamental foundation of our strong democracy, secure nation, and sound economy, and of the hopes and aspirations of generations of children. I am particularly grateful for the time Secretary Rice devoted to listening to our concerns, and the genuineness of our shared commitment to providing all young people access to a high-quality public education.

The report rightly acknowledges that "Public education is an essential institution in America's quest to provide equality of opportunity and to ensure that social and economic mobility are available to all children, regardless of circumstances. It is not hyperbole to say that a robust system of public schools is essential to U.S. democracy."

Regrettably, some elements of this report actually undermine this vital institution. The report casts public schools in the worst possible light while ignoring facts to the contrary. It correctly states that parents should have great academic choices for their children, but certain recommendations may actually limit those choices. It advances recommendations that lack evidence of effectiveness while ignoring the lessons of high-achieving, fully public education systems in the United States and elsewhere. The report advocates privatization, competition, and market-based approaches that, while compelling, have not worked in a scalable and sustainable way either here or abroad. Therefore, I must respectfully offer this partial dissent.

The report rightly emphasizes the need for all students to have access to great schools and the opportunity to develop higher-order knowledge and skills. Yet by promoting policies like the current top-down, standardized test–driven accountability that has narrowed the curriculum and reinforced the teaching of lower-level skills, which President Obama correctly criticized in his 2012 State of the Union address, it does the opposite. The report goes to great lengths to blame a current generation of educators for their assumed institutional resistance to innovation when, in fact, the problem is less about an opposition to change than it is about too much churn and change. This adds to disrespect and the sharp demoralization of our current teaching force—something that is never seen in the countries that outcompete us. We ask teachers to do a lot, and while we have the responsibility to remove those who do not belong in the profession, we have just as great a responsibility to provide the tools, conditions, and support to the vast majority of teachers who do. Public schools have been buffeted by so many "silver bullet," top-down solutions and unprecedented austerity measures that sound reforms with the potential to drive system-wide student success have not been consistently and equitably implemented.

Vouchers and charters have not proven themselves to be sustainable or systemic ways to improve our schools. They will, instead, deplete badly needed resources from the public schools that educate nearly 90 percent of our students. We are concerned, therefore, that their favorable mention in this report—without accompanying comments about the problems inherent in each—could have the effect of "walking away" from the public responsibility and sufficient funding for public schooling. Decades of independent research show that vouchers do not improve outcomes for children who receive them or drive improvements in nearby neighborhood schools. Recent polling on communities of color and public school reform (conducted for the NAACP, the National Council of La Raza, and others) showed that parents favor improving, not closing, struggling schools. Moreover, the countries that have enacted voucher systems, such as Chile, have not seen the improvements in achievement predicted by advocates. Chile, in fact, is the most socioeconomically segregated country regarding education opportunities, according to the OECD.

We applaud the support expressed for the Common Core State Standards, and we strongly agree that we must have high expectations for all children. It is incumbent upon all of us to ensure that our students and schools are provided the resources they need to meet those high expectations. We are pleased therefore to see incorporated in the report the recognition that schools need greater resources and that there needs to be an integration and alignment between those resources, policy, implementation, and support. Experience—both recent and long—has shown that we set our students and our schools up for failure if we advocate for higher standards and do not provide the funding and other supports needed to achieve them.

The report rightly decries the gaps in achievement between disadvantaged children and their more-advantaged peers, but it does not make a strong recommendation to address closing the corresponding gap in education funding and resources. It rehashes the too-familiar canard that education resources outpace results, but makes no note of schools' growing costs associated with educating all children (including students with special needs or living in poverty) and rampant teacher turnover.

Educating our nation's children only works when it is viewed as—and lived as—a shared responsibility. This report repeatedly moves away from that concept, instead placing inordinate responsibility for school improvement on individual teachers and advocating educational approaches, such as vouchers and charter schools, that are disconnected from public systems. Our belief is that improvements that benefit all children can be achieved only through systemic structural changes. And when structural changes are made in education, the people who do the work must have a say. We are pleased that the report acknowledges, by its inclusion, that collective bargaining is a tool in creating true education reform. It can be and has been used to create more school autonomy, but we are mindful that these proposals work only when there is real collaboration, worker voice, and real support by a school system for its schools.

Through collaborative efforts and shared responsibility, we must focus on the two primary linchpins of educational attainment: what students need to succeed, and what their teachers need to facilitate success. The components of such an approach include curricula, teacher development and evaluation, meaningful accountability measures, and neighborhood schools, as outlined in AFT's Quality Agenda: http://www.aft.org/newspubs/press/qualityagenda.cfm.

In this country, no other public service essential to the nation's well-being—not law enforcement, firefighting, or the armed forces—has forsaken being a public entity. Public education has been a cornerstone of democracy and a means of acculturation for generations of Americans, as well as a crucial vehicle by which those generations have not simply dreamed their dreams but achieved them. A move away from that public system could do greater harm to our national security and common bonds than doing nothing at all.

Randi Weingarten
joined by Carole Artigiani, Linda Darling-Hammond,
and Stephen M. Walt

Endnotes

1. Deloitte, Oracle, and the Manufacturing Institute, "People and Profitability: A time for change," 2009, http://www.deloitte.com/assets/Dcom-UnitedStates/Local%20 Assets/Documents/us_pip_peoplemanagementreport_100509.pdf.
2. Aerospace Industries Association, "America's Technical Workforce Crisis," 2011.
3. Mission: Readiness, "Ready, Willing and Unable to Serve," 2009, http://cdn.mission-readiness.org/MR-Ready-Willing-Unable.pdf.
4. Ibid.
5. Government Accountability Office, *Department of State: Comprehensive Plan Needed to Address Persistent Foreign Language Shortfalls*, Report to the Subcommittee on Oversight of Government Management, the Federal Workforce, and the District of Columbia, Committee on Homeland Security and Governmental Affairs, U.S. Senate, 111th Congress (2009), http://www.gao.gov/new.items/d09955.pdf.
6. Nicole Stoops, "Educational Attainment in the United States: 2003," Current Population Report P20-550 (Washington, DC: U.S. Census Bureau, 2004), http://www.census.gov/prod/2004pubs/p20-550.pdf; Chris Chapman, Jennifer Laird, and Angelina KewalRamani, "Trends in High School Dropout and Completion Rates in the United States: 1972–2008" (Washington, DC: National Center for Education Statistics, 2010), http://nces.ed.gov/pubs2011/2011012.pdf.
7. Sabrina Tavernise, "Education Gap Grows Between Rich and Poor, Studies Say," *New York Times*, February 9, 2012, http://www.nytimes.com/2012/02/10/education/education-gap-grows-between-rich-and-poor-studies-show.html.
8. Michael Spence, "The Impact of Globalization on Income and Employment," *Foreign Affairs*, vol. 90, no. 4, July/August 2011.
9. Mission: Readiness, "Ready, Willing and Unable to Serve."
10. Ibid.
11. Only 50 percent of high school dropouts complete their first three years of service, compared to about 80 percent of graduates. W. S. Sellman, "Predicting Readiness for Military Service: How Enlistment Standards are Established," prepared for the National Assessment Governing Board, September 2004.
12. Christina Theokas, "Shut Out of the Military: Today's High School Education Doesn't Mean You're Ready for Today's Army," Education Trust, December 2010, http://www.edtrust.org/dc/publication/shut-out-of-the-military.
13. Ibid.
14. National Science Board, "Science and Engineering Indicators 2010," NSB 10-01 (Arlington, VA: National Science Foundation, 2010), table 2-36, http://www.nsf.gov/statistics/seind10/pdf/seind10.pdf.
15. "Statistical Abstract of the United States: 2012" (Washington, DC: U.S. Census Bureau, 2011), table 810, http://www.census.gov/compendia/statab/2012/tables/12s0811.pdf.
16. National Science Foundation, Science and Engineering Indicators 2012, http://www.nsf.gov/statistics/seind12/c2/c2h.htm.

17. General William Wallace, Commanding General, United States Army Training and Doctrine Command (TRADOC), from 2005 to December 2008.

18. Michael T. Flynn, Matt Pottinger, and Paul D. Batchelor, "Fixing Intel: A Blueprint for Making Intelligence Relevant in Afghanistan," Center for New American Security, January 2010, http://www.cnas.org/files/documents/publications/AfghanIntel_Flynn_Jan2010_code507_voices.pdf.

19. Fourteen U.S. intelligence agencies recently released a report on cyber espionage that found that it is a "growing and persistent" threat. At the release, the U.S. counterespionage chief, Robert Bryant, said, "This is a national, long-term, strategic threat to the United States of America. This is an issue where failure is not an option." The report estimated that cyber spying cost the United States $50 billion in 2009 alone. Siobhan Gorman, "China Singled Out for Cyberspying," *Wall Street Journal*, November 4, 2011, http://online.wsj.com/article/SB10001424052970203716204577015540198801540.html#ixzz1dK3TgTEm.

20. Statement of Gregory C. Wilshusen, director, information security issues, *Cybersecurity: Continued Attention Needed to Protect Our Nation's Critical Infrastructure, Before the Subcommittee on Oversight and Investigations*, Committee on Energy and Commerce, House of Representatives, 112th Congress (2011).

21. Interview with Timothy McKnight, chief information security officer of Northrop Grumman Corporation, in "The Stand: Cybersecurity," 1105 Government Information Group, accessed March 7, 2012, http://washingtontechnology.com/pages/custom/stand-cybersecurity.aspx.

22. Government Accountability Office, *Department of State: Comprehensive Plan Needed to Address Persistent Foreign Language Shortfalls.*

23. Ibid.

24. Paula Caligiuri et al., "Training, Developing, and Assessing Cross-Cultural Competence in Military Personnel," Technical Report 1284 (Washington: United States Army Research Institute for the Behavioral and Social Sciences, 2011), http://www.defense-culture.org/researchfile/Caligiuri_Training_Developing_Assessing.pdf.

25. Memorandum from Secretary of Defense Leon Panetta, "Language Skills, Regional Expertise, and Cultural Capabilities in the Department of Defense," August 10, 2011, http://flenj.org/Docs/2011-AUG-Leon-Panetta-Memo.pdf. To address this need, the Department of Defense established Project GO (Global Officers) to teach language and culture to college students, and created a website dedicated to helping service members develop their cultural competence. The Air Force also created a website that offers free courses in cross-cultural awareness.

26. Elizabeth Mendes, "In U.S., Optimism About Future for Youth Reaches All-Time Low," *USA Today*/Gallup poll, May 2, 2011, http://www.gallup.com/poll/147350/Optimism-Future-Youth-Reaches-Time-Low.aspx. A recent *New York Times* article said that Americans have less ability to move upward in society than peers in other countries. It quoted a Brookings economist, Isabel V. Sawhill, saying, "It's becoming conventional wisdom that the U.S. does not have as much mobility as most other advanced countries." Jason DeParle, "Harder for Americans to Rise From Lower Rungs," *New York Times*, January 4, 2012, http://www.nytimes.com/2012/01/05/us/harder-for-americans-to-rise-from-lower-rungs.html?_r=2.

27. The achievement gap between rich and poor students has grown in recent decades and the college completion gap has grown by about 50 percent, according to studies cited by the *New York Times*. Tavernise, "Education Gap Grows Between Rich and Poor, Studies Say."

28. On NAEP, only 27 percent of fourth graders, 22 percent of eighth graders, and 24 percent of twelfth graders performed at proficient or above on the civics NAEP in 2010. "The Nation's Report Card: Civics 2010," NCES 2011-466 (Washington, DC:

National Center for Education Statistics, 2011), http://nces.ed.gov/nationsreportcard/pubs/main2010/2011466.asp#section1.

29. "NAEP Question Tool," National Center for Education Statistics, http://nces.ed.gov/nationsreportcard/itmrlsx/search.aspx?subject=civics. Note: The Task Force looked at the proportion of students who successfully answered the questions described in this paragraph.

30. Hyon B. Shin and Robert A. Kominski, "Language Use in the United States: 2007," ACS-12 (Washington, DC: U.S. Census Bureau, 2010), http://www.census.gov/prod/2010pubs/acs-12.pdf.

31. "Statistical Abstract of the United States: 2011" (Washington, DC: U.S. Census Bureau, 2011), table 52, http://www.census.gov/compendia/statab/2011/tables/11s0052.pdf. In the United States, the number of schools teaching foreign languages is falling: elementary schools from 31 percent in 1997 to 25 percent in 2008, and secondary schools from 86 percent in 1997 to 79 percent in 2008. Nancy C. Rhodes and Ingrid Pufahl, "Foreign Language Teaching in U.S. Schools: Results of a National Survey," Center for Applied Linguistics, November 2008, http://www.cal.org/projects/flsurvey.html.

32. Statistics Canada, http://www12.statcan.gc.ca/census-recensement/2006/dp-pd/tbt/Rp-eng.cfm?LANG=E&APATH=3&DETAIL=0&DIM=0&FL=A&FREE=0&GC=0&GID=0&GK=0&GRP=1&PID=89188&PRID=0&PTYPE=88971,97154&S=0&SHOWALL=0&SUB=0&Temporal=2006&THEME=70-&VID=0&VNAMEE=&VNAMEF; European Commission, http://ec.europa.eu/languages/languages-of-europe/eurobarometer-survey_en.htm.

33. "The NAEP Glossary of Terms," http://nationsreportcard.gov/glossary.asp.

34. "The Nation's Report Card: Reading 2009" (Washington, DC: National Center for Education Statistics, 2010), http://nces.ed.gov/nationsreportcard/pdf/main2009/2010458.pdf; "The Nation's Report Card: Grade 4 Results" (Washington, DC: National Center for Education Statistics, 2009), http://nationsreportcard.gov/math_2009/gr4_state.asp?subtab_id=Tab_1&tab_id=tab1#tabsContainer; "The Nation's Report Card: Grade 8 Results" (Washington, DC: National Center for Education Statistics, 2009), http://nationsreportcard.gov/math_2009/gr8_national.asp?tab_id=tab2&subtab_id=Tab_1#tabsContainer.

35. National Assessment of Educational Progress, "What Does the NAEP Mathematics Assessment Measure?" http://nces.ed.gov/nationsreportcard/mathematics/whatmeasure.asp.

36. National Assessment of Educational Progress, "What Does the NAEP Reading Assessment Measure?" http://nces.ed.gov/nationsreportcard/reading/whatmeasure.asp; National Assessment of Educational Progress, "What Does the NAEP Science Assessment Measure?" http://nces.ed.gov/nationsreportcard/science/whatmeasure.asp.

37. The achievement gap separating white and black students in reading—at both the fourth- and eighth-grade levels—has shrunk only slightly since 1992. For eighth graders, the gap shrank only slightly, from thirty points in 1992 to twenty-seven points in 2009. For fourth graders, the gap narrowed more, from thirty-two in 1992 to twenty-five in 2009. In math, the results are similar. For eighth graders, the gap shrank from thirty in 1992 to twenty-seven in 2009. For fourth graders, the gap shrank from thirty-two in 1992 to twenty-five in 2009.

38. "The Nation's Report Card: Grade 4 Results" (Washington, DC: National Center for Education Statistics, 2009), http://nationsreportcard.gov/math_2009/gr4_state.asp?subtab_id=Tab_1&tab_id=tab1#tabsContainer.

39. In fourth-grade reading, the difference between the five states with the highest standards and the five with the lowest standards was comparable to the difference between basic and proficient performance on NAEP. "Mapping State Proficiency Standards onto the NAEP Scales: Variation and Change in State Standards for Reading and

Mathematics, 2005–2009," NCES 2011-458 (Washington, DC: National Center for Education Statistics, 2011), http://nces.ed.gov/nationsreportcard/pdf/studies/2011458.pdf.

40. 1.3 million school-age American children have parents who are in active duty, reserves, or the National Guard. This is about double the number who attend schools in New York City, America's largest public school district. Of these students, 76 percent attend regular public schools, about 10 percent attend private schools, and only about 8 percent attend Department of Defense schools. Data provided by Mary M. Keller, president and CEO of the Military Child Education Coalition.

41. When General George Casey became chief of staff of the army, he and his wife Sheila Casey spent a hundred days traveling the country and talking to military families. Mrs. Casey said that worries about schools came up everywhere she went. "We have an epidemic out there," she said. "It touches a lot of people." Interview, August 17, 2011.

42. Data provided by Mary M. Keller, president and CEO of the Military Child Education Coalition, on August 16, 2011.

43. M. Janosz, I. Archambault, J. Morizot, and L. S. Pagani, "School Engagement Trajectories and Their Differential Predictive Relations to Dropout," *Journal of Social Issues*, vol. 64, no. 1, March 2008.

44. The U.S. Department of Education reports that the average freshman graduation rate (AFGR), which is an estimate of the students who graduate in four years, is 75 percent. Chapman et al., "Trends in High School Dropout and Completion Rates in the United States: 1972–2008," table 13, http://nces.ed.gov/pubs2011/dropout08/tables/table_13.asp.

45. The graduation rate in the United States is 62 percent for black students and 63 percent for Hispanic students, compared with 74.5 percent for white students and 90 percent for Asian students. "Public School Graduates and Dropouts from the Common Core of Data: School Year 2008–09," NCES 2011-312 (Washington, DC: National Center for Education Statistics, 2011), table 2, http://nces.ed.gov/pubs2011/graduates/tables/table_02.asp.

46. In the last year of available data, from 2008 to 2009, states' high school graduation rates range from a low of 56 percent in Nevada to a high of 91 percent in Wisconsin. "Public School Graduates and Dropouts," table 1, http://nces.ed.gov/pubs2011/graduates/tables/table_01.asp.

47. "College Readiness: Benchmarks Met," ACT, 2008, http://www.act.org/newsroom/data/2008/benchmarks.html.

48. Ibid.

49. "43 Percent of 2011 College-Bound Seniors Met SAT College and Career Readiness Benchmark," College Board press release, September 2011, http://press.collegeboard.org/releases/2011/43-percent-2011-college-bound-seniors-met-sat-college-and-career-readiness-benchmark.

50. "The Condition of Education 2011: Indicator 22, Remedial Counseling," NCES 2011-033 (Washington, DC: National Center for Education Statistics, 2011), http://nces.ed.gov/programs/coe/pdf/coe_rmc.pdf.

51. "Paying Double: Inadequate High Schools and Community College Remediation," Alliance for Excellent Education Issue Brief, August 2006, http://www.all4ed.org/files/archive/publications/remediation.pdf.

52. Chapman et al., "Trends in High School Dropout and Completion Rates in the United States: 1972–2008."

53. Bureau of Labor Statistics, Current Population Survey, "Education Pays," http://www.bls.gov/emp/ep_chart_001.htm; "Dynamics of Economic Well-Being: Poverty 2004–2006" (Washington: U.S. Census Bureau, 2011), table 1b, http://www.census.gov/hhes/www/poverty/publications/dynamics04/table1b.pdf.

54. Andrew Sum, Ishwar Khatiwada, and Joseph McLaughlin, "The Consequences of Dropping Out of High School," Center for Labor Market Studies, Northeastern University, 2009, http://hdl.handle.net/2047/d20000596.

55. Dropouts themselves report that they quit school for five main reasons: classes were not interesting; they had missed too much school and could not catch up; they spent time with friends who were not interested in school; they had too much freedom and not enough discipline in their lives; and/or they were failing school. John M. Bridgeland, John J. Dilulio Jr., and Karen Burke Morison, "The Silent Epidemic: Perspectives of High School Dropouts" Civic Enterprises, March 2006, http://www.ignitelearning.com/pdf/TheSilentEpidemic3-06FINAL.pdf.

56. OECD, "Comparing Countries and Economies' Performance," figure 1, http://www.pisa.oecd.org/dataoecd/54/12/46643496.pdf.

57. "Highlights from PISA 2009," NCES 2011-004 (Washington, DC: National Center for Education Statistics, 2010), http://nces.ed.gov/pubs2011/2011004.pdf.

58. Ibid.

59. In reading, students in Shanghai had an average score of 556, against 500 among those in the United States; in math, an average of 600, versus 487; and in science, an average of 575, against 502. "Highlights from PISA 2009."

60. Sam Dillon, "Top Test Scores from Shanghai Stun Educators," *New York Times*, December 7, 2010, http://www.nytimes.com/2010/12/07/education/07education.html?scp=1&sq=shanghai%20test&st=cse.

61. Erik Hanushek, Paul E. Peterson, and Ludger Woessmann, "Teaching Math to the Talented," *Education Next*, vol. 11, no. 1, winter 2011, http://educationnext.org/teaching-math-to-the-talented.

62. Gary W. Phillips, "The Second Derivative: International Benchmarks in Mathematics for U.S. States and School Districts" American Institutes for Research, June 2009, http://www.air.org/files/International_Benchmarks1.pdf.

63. Jay P. Greene and Josh B. McGee, "When the Best Is Mediocre," *Education Next*, vol. 12, no. 1, winter 2012, http://educationnext.org/when-the-best-is-mediocre.

64. Thomas D. Snyder and Sally A. Dillow, *Digest of Education Statistics, 2010*, NCES 2011-015 (Washington, DC: National Center for Education Statistics, 2011), table 421, http://nces.ed.gov/programs/digest/d10/tables/dt10_421.asp.

65. OECD, *Lessons from PISA for the United States: Strong Performers and Successful Reformers in Education*, 2011, http://www.oecd-ilibrary.org/education/lessons-from-pisa-for-the-united-states_9789264096660-en.

66. OECD Stat Extras, Child Wellbeing, http://stats.oecd.org/Index.aspx?DataSetCode=INEQUALITY.

67. Hanushek et al., "Teaching Math to the Talented."

68. Bobby D. Rampey, Gloria S. Dion, and Patricia L. Donahue, "The Nation's Report Card: Trends in Academic Progress in Reading and Mathematics 2008," NCES 2009-479 (Washington, DC: National Center for Education Statistics, 2009), http://nces.ed.gov/nationsreportcard/pubs/main2008/2009479.asp; "Fast Facts," National Center for Education Statistics, http://nces.ed.gov/fastfacts/display.asp?id=66.

69. Ibid.

70. Snyder and Dillow, *Digest of Education Statistics: 2010*, table 68, http://nces.ed.gov/programs/digest/d10/tables/dt10_068.asp?referrer=report.

71. In an interview with the Task Force, U.S. Department of Education officials said that between 1999 and 2008, the number of public elementary school teachers increased from 1,602,000 to 1,725,000, and the number of special education teachers increased from 210,000 to 230,000. For secondary school teachers, the total grew from 1,401,000 to 1,680,000 and the special education teacher count grew from 99,000 to 165,000.

72. OECD, *Education at a Glance 2011: OECD Indicators*, 2011, p. 218, table B1.1a, http://www.oecd.org/dataoecd/61/2/48631582.pdf. In an interview with the Task Force, U.S. Department of Education officials said these are not exact apples-to-apples comparisons since each participating OECD country self-reports and has different methods of measurement, but they noted that if the report adjusted for these reporting differences, the United States would still be spending more than average.

73. Ulrich Boser, "Return on Educational Investment: A District-by-District Evaluation of U.S. Educational Productivity," January 2011, Center on American Progress, http://www.americanprogress.org/issues/2011/01/pdf/dwwroi.pdf.

74. Ibid.

75. Albert Shanker, op-ed, *Wall Street Journal*, October 2, 1989.

76. Marguerite Roza, *Educational Economics: Where Do School Funds Go?* (Washington, DC: Urban Institute Press, 2010), p. 7.

77. OECD, *Lessons from PISA*.

78. "The Condition of Education 2011," table A-35-2, http://nces.ed.gov/programs/coe/tables/table-sft-2.asp.

79. Calculation based on "The Condition of Education 2011," tables A-35-2 and A-2-2.

80. Marguerite Roza, Kacey Guin, Betheny Gross, and Scott Deburgomaster, "Do Districts Fund Schools Fairly?" *Education Next*, vol. 7, no. 4, fall 2007, http://educationnext.org/do-districts-fund-schools-fairly.

81. "Report to the President: Prepare and Inspire: K-12 Education in Science, Technology, Engineering, and Math (STEM) for American's Future," Executive Office of the President, President's Council of Advisers on Science and Technology, September 2010, p. 32, http://www.whitehouse.gov/sites/default/files/microsites/ostp/pcast-stemed-report.pdf.

82. "Research and development expenditure (% of GDP)," World Bank, http://data.worldbank.org/indicator/GB.XPD.RSDV.GD.ZS.

83. "Fast Facts," National Center for Education Statistics, http://nces.ed.gov/fastfacts/display.asp?id=46.

84. "The Condition of Education 2011," table A-36-1, http://nces.ed.gov/programs/coe/tables/table-tot-1.asp.

85. "Salary Schedule Effective May 19, 2008: Certified Teachers Schedule," New York City Department of Education, http://schools.nyc.gov/NR/rdonlyres/72DE1FF1-EDFC-40D7-9D61-831014B39D1E/0/TeacherSalarySchedule20083.pdf.

86. Robert Gordon, Thomas J. Kane, and Douglas O. Staiger, "Identifying Effective Teachers Using Performance on the Job," Hamilton Project white paper 2006-01, Brookings Institution, April 2006. A more recent study, covered by the *New York Times* in January 2012, found that effective elementary and middle-school teachers have wide-ranging, long-term effects on students' lives. They not only improve students' academic performance; their students are also less likely to become teenage parents, more likely to go to college, and more likely to earn higher incomes as adults. See Annie Lowrey, "Big Study Links Good Teachers to Lasting Gain," *New York Times*, January 6, 2012, http://www.nytimes.com/2012/01/06/education/big-study-links-good-teachers-to-lasting-gain.html?_r=3&ref=education.

87. OECD, *Lessons from PISA*.

88. Byron Auguste, Paul Kihn, and Matt Miller, "Closing the Talent Gap: Attracting and Retaining Top-Third Graduates to Careers in Teaching," McKinsey & Company, 2012, http://www.mckinsey.com/clientservice/Social_Sector/our_practices/Education/Knowledge_Highlights/~/media/Reports/SSO/Closing_the_talent_gap.ashx.

89. Auguste et al., "Closing the Talent Gap"; Caroline M. Hoxby and Andrew Leigh, "Wage Distortion: Why America's Top Women College Graduates Aren't Teaching," *Education Next*, vol. 4, no. 2, spring 2005, http://educationnext.org/wagedistortion.

90. Gordon et al., "Identifying Effective Teachers."
91. Auguste et al., "Closing the Talent Gap."
92. Ibid.
93. OECD, *Lessons from PISA*.
94. "Common Core State Initiative Standards," http://www.corestandards.org.
95. David T. Conley, Kathryn V. Drummond, Alicia de Gonzalez, Jennifer Rooseboom, and Odile Stou, "Reaching the Goal: The Applicability and Importance of the Common Core State Standards to College and Career Readiness," Educational Policy Improvement Center, 2011, https://www.epiconline.org/files/pdf/ReachingtheGoal-FullReport.pdf.
96. Annually, TFA selects a corps of about six thousand teachers and sends them to high-needs school districts across the country. Source: Wendy Kopp interview.
97. A new study by MDRC that analyzed twenty-one thousand students who applied for admission at more than one hundred new small schools in New York that replaced large, failing schools found that 67.9 percent of the students who were admitted graduated four years later, compared to 59.3 percent who were not admitted and went to larger schools instead. This is true for all students studied, regardless of race, family income, or their previous academic performance. Howard S. Bloom and Rebecca Unterman, "Sustained Positive Effects on Graduation Rates Produced by New York City's Small Public High Schools of Choice," January 2012, http://www.mdrc.org/publications/614/overview.html.
98. A new study, "Charter Schools and Achievement," analyzed previous studies on charter schools and found that there is some variation in the quality of charter schools, but there is "ample evidence that charter elementary schools on average outperform traditional public schools in both reading and math, and that charter middle schools outperform in math." Julian R. Betts and Y. Emily Tang, "Charter Schools and Achievement," Center on Reinventing Public Education Research Brief, October 2011, http://www.crpe.org/cs/crpe/download/csr_files/brief_NCRSP_BettsTang_Oct11.pdf.
99. Ibid.
100. "The 2011 State of Public Education in New Orleans," Cowen Institute for Public Education Initiatives at Tulane University, July 2011, http://www.coweninstitute.com/wp-content/uploads/2011/07/2011-SPENO-report.pdf.
101. For example, Lou Gerstner, interview by Fareed Zakaria, "Former IBM CEO on state of US worker," *Fareed Zakaria GPS*, CNN, October 29, 2010, http://www.cnn.com/video/#/video/us/2010/10/29/gps.gerstner.us.workers.cnn.
102. "Employment Projections: 2010-2020 Summary" (Washington, DC: U.S. Bureau of Labor Statistics, 2012), http://www.bls.gov/news.release/ecopro.nro.htm.
103. Anthony P. Carnevale, Nicole Smith, and Jeff Strohl, "Help Wanted: Projections of Jobs and Education Requirements Through 2018," June 2010, http://www9.georgetown.edu/grad/gppi/hpi/cew/pdfs/FullReport.pdf.
104. Ibid.
105. Ibid.
106. James Manyika, Susan Lund, Byron Auguste, Lenny Mendonca, Tim Welsh, and Sreenivas Ramaswamy, "An economy that works: Job creation and America's future," McKinsey & Company, 2011, http://www.mckinsey.com/Insights/MGI/Research/Labor_Markets/An_economy_that_works_for_US_job_creation.
107. "Getting Ahead—Staying Ahead: Helping America's Workforce Succeed in the 21st Century," Business Roundtable, December 2009, http://businessroundtable.org/uploads/studies-reports/downloads/BRT_Getting_Ahead_online_version_1.pdf.
108. Ibid.

109. Manyika et al., "An economy that works."

110. John Bridgeland, Jessica Milano, and Elyse Rosenblum, "Across the Great Divide: Perspectives of CEOs and College Presidents on America's High Education and Skills Gap," Civic Enterprises, March 2011, http://www.civicenterprises.net/reports/across_the_great_divide.pdf.

111. "Framework for 21st Century Learning," Partnership for 21st Century Skills, http://www.p21.org/overview/skills-framework.

112. For a good summary of the main frameworks for twenty-first-century learning, see C. Dede, "Comparing Frameworks for 21st Century Skills," in *21st Century Skills*, eds. J. Bellanca and R. Brandt (Bloomington, IN: Solution Tree Press, 2010), pp. 51–76.

113. "Chapter 11: Foresight—and Hindsight," in *The 9/11 Commission Report* (Washington, DC: The National Commission on Terrorist Attacks Upon the United States, 2004), http://www.911commission.gov/report/911Report.pdf.

114. The states with the largest presence of military-connected children and youth (active duty, National Guard, and reserves) are, in order of number: Texas, Virginia, California, North Carolina, Georgia, Washington, Florida, Hawaii, Kentucky, Colorado, South Carolina, Kansas, Maryland, Oklahoma, and New York. "Military Child Education Coalition," http://www.militarychild.org.

115. The National Commission on Excellence in Education, "A Nation at Risk: The Imperative for Educational Reform" (Washington, DC: Government Printing Office, 1983), http://reagan.procon.org/sourcefiles/a-nation-at-risk-reagan-april-1983.pdf.

116. Ibid.

Task Force Members

Task Force members are asked to join a consensus signifying that they endorse "the general policy thrust and judgments reached by the group, though not necessarily every finding and recommendation." They participate in the Task Force in their individual, not institutional, capacities.

Carole Artigiani is founder and president emerita of Global Kids, Inc. (GK), an educational organization dedicated to assuring that urban youth achieve academic success and leadership in their communities and on the global stage. Operating in New York City and Washington, DC, it involves over fifteen thousand students and educators each year and millions more through youth-produced online media. GK's programs are grounded in the belief that youth have the will and capacity to understand and address complex global issues, and that learning to take action develops twenty-first-century skills and counters cynicism, common among young people in underserved communities, about their power to shape their futures and influence policies that affect their lives. Annually, over 90 percent of participants graduate from high school and go to college. Artigiani holds a BA in history from Notre Dame College and an MA in women's history from Sarah Lawrence College. A former teacher and college administrator, she has been cited as a distinguished alumna by both of her alma maters, a Purpose Prize fellow, and Outstanding Educator by the Anne Frank Foundation. She serves on the boards of GK and the Institute of Play and is a member of the Council on Foreign Relations.

Craig R. Barrett received BS, MS, and PhD degrees in materials science from Stanford University. He was a Fulbright fellow at the Danish Technical University and a NATO postdoctoral fellow at the National Physical Laboratory in England. Barrett joined Intel in 1974 and was promoted to president in 1997, CEO in 1998, and chairman in 2005, a post he held until 2009. Barrett is a leading advocate for improving education and is a vocal spokesman for the value technology can provide in raising social and economic standards globally. He chairs Achieve, Change the Equation, Dossia, the Skolkovo Foundation Council, the Arizona Ready Education Council, and BASIS School, Inc.; co-chairs the Lawrence Berkeley National Laboratory advisory board; vice chairs Science Foundation Arizona and the National Forest Foundation; and is on the boards of Society for Science and the Public, K12 Inc., and the Arizona Commerce Authority. Barrett formerly served as chair of the UN Global Alliance for Information and Communication Technologies and Development and the National Academy of Engineering; co-chaired the Business Coalition for Student Achievement and National Innovation Initiative Leadership Council; and served on the board of the U.S. Council for International Business and on the Clinton Global Initiative education advisory board.

Richard Barth was made CEO and president of the Knowledge is Power Program (KIPP) Foundation in December 2005. Over the past six years, he has overseen the significant growth of the network from 45 to 109 schools, dramatically expanded KIPP's leadership development programs, advocated for high-performing charter schools on Capitol Hill, and secured more than $190 million in new, long-term philanthropic commitments, including more than $75 million from the federal government. Barth came to KIPP from Edison Schools, where he served as president of district partnerships and managed school partnerships serving over forty thousand students. Prior to joining Edison, Barth was one of the founding staff members of Teach For America. He earned a BA in American history from Harvard University and is an Aspen Institute–NewSchools fellow. He currently sits on the board of directors of 50CAN, the Broad Center for the Management of School Systems, and Be the Change, Inc., and is president of the KIPP Foundation board of directors.

Edith L. Bartley is the director of government affairs for UNCF, for which she leads and manages government affairs federal policy work. Bartley has fifteen years of public policy and advocacy experience working for both the nonprofit and private sectors on a variety of issues, including education, affordable housing, international terrorism, energy, and foreign affairs. She has worked in five congressional offices and served as a congressional speechwriter and legislative aide. She attended law school at the University of Missouri and was a visiting student at Georgetown Law Center, graduating in 2001. She has a BA from Hampton University. Prior to joining UNCF, Bartley worked as a member of the government affairs team of Thelen Reid & Priest law firm in Washington, DC. She also worked as an advocate for the National Council of State Housing Agencies. Since 1998, Bartley has worked as an advocate for victims of international terrorism, raising the sensitivity to this issue in both chambers of the U.S. Congress as a result of the death of her father and brother in the August 7, 1998, al-Qaeda bombing of the U.S. Embassy in Nairobi, Kenya. Bartley has appeared on national and international news networks including CNN, NPR, MSNBC, and Fox.

Gaston Caperton is president of the College Board and a former two-term governor of West Virginia. After a successful business career in finance and insurance, Caperton was elected governor in 1988 and quickly revolutionized the state's education system. Under his leadership, the average West Virginian teacher's salary rose from forty-ninth lowest in the nation to thirty-first; he launched one of the country's earliest and most comprehensive basic computer skills initiatives; and he invested more than $800 million in building, modernizing, and improving school facilities throughout the state. Since 1999, Caperton has served as the eighth president of the College Board, transforming the century-old institution into a mission-driven, student-first operation that promotes college success and opportunity for all Americans. During his thirteen years of leadership, the College Board has touched the lives of students in nearly twenty-seven thousand high schools and colleges, promoted the importance of writing by adding a writing section to the SAT exam, and doubled the number of students succeeding in advanced placement classes. Over the course of twenty-plus years in government and education, Caperton has chaired the Democratic Governor's Association, received ten honorary doctoral degrees, and was presented with the James Bryant Conant Award for his significant contributions to the quality of education in the United States.

Linda Darling-Hammond is the Charles E. Ducommun professor of education at Stanford University, where she launched the Stanford Center for Opportunity Policy in Education and the School Redesign

Network and has served as faculty sponsor for the Stanford Teacher Education Program. She is a former president of the American Educational Research Association and member of the National Academy of Education. In 2008–2009, she headed President Barack Obama's education policy transition team. Her research, teaching, and policy work focus on issues of school reform, teacher quality, and educational equity. Among Darling-Hammond's more than three hundred publications are *The Flat World and Education: How America's Commitment to Equity Will Determine Our Future* and *Powerful Teacher Education: Lessons from Exemplary Programs*. Among recent recognitions, she is the recipient of the 2011 Brock International Prize in Education and the 2009 McGraw Hill Prize for Innovation in Education.

Jonah M. Edelman is cofounder and CEO of Stand for Children, the nation's most influential political voice for students. Stand for Children exists to ensure all students graduate from high school prepared for, and with access to, college. This year, it was a catalyst in the passage of key laws to improve public education in seven states. Edelman's personal stand for children began during college when he taught a six-year-old bilingual child to read. He went on to found a mentorship program for middle school students and then served as an administrator of an enrichment program for children living in public housing, Leadership Education and Athletics in Partnership. Edelman is continuing a long family line of service to community. His grandparents, Arthur and Maggie Wright, started their town's first home for the aged and took in twenty-two foster children. Edelman's parents, Marian Wright Edelman and Peter Edelman, have stood up for civil rights, equal opportunity, and children's well-being through their careers. Edelman graduated from Yale University in 1992 and attended Oxford University on a Rhodes scholarship, where in three years he earned master and doctor of philosophy degrees in politics. In 1996, Edelman helped organize Stand for Children's historic founding rally—attended by over three hundred thousand people—in Washington, DC. Edelman was recognized on Time.com as one of the nation's top eleven education activists for 2011.

Roland Fryer Jr. is the Robert M. Beren professor of economics at Harvard University, a research associate at the National Bureau of Economic Research, founder and principal investigator of the Education Innovation Laboratory at Harvard, and a former junior fellow in the

Harvard Society of Fellows. At thirty, he became the youngest African American to receive tenure from Harvard. He has been awarded a Sloan research fellowship, a Faculty Early Career Development Award from the National Science Foundation, and the inaugural Alphonse Fletcher Award. Fryer served as chief equality officer at the New York City Department of Education from 2007 to 2008. He developed and implemented several innovative ideas on student motivation and teacher pay-for-performance concepts. He won a Titanium Lion at the Cannes Lions International Advertising Festival for the Million Motivation Campaign. Fryer has published papers on the racial achievement gap, causes and consequences of distinctively black names, affirmative action, the impact of the crack cocaine epidemic, historically black colleges and universities, and acting white. Fryer is a 2009 recipient of a Presidential Early Career Award for Scientists and Engineers. He appears on the 2009 Time 100, *Time* magazine's annual list of the world's most influential people. In 2011, he was awarded a MacArthur "genius" grant from the John D. and Catherine T. MacArthur Foundation.

Ann M. Fudge is the retired chairman and CEO of Young & Rubicam Brands, a global network of marketing communications companies. Prior to Young & Rubicam Brands, Fudge served as president of the $5 billion beverages, desserts, and Post division of Kraft Foods. She has served on the management committees of and managed many businesses, including Maxwell House Coffee, Gevalia Kaffe, Kool Aid, Crystal Light, Post cereals, Jell-O desserts, and Altoids. Before joining Kraft Foods, she spent nine years at General Mills. She serves as chair of the U.S. programs advisory board of the Gates Foundation and is a trustee of the Rockefeller Foundation, Brookings Institution, and Morehouse College. She also serves on the board of directors of General Electric, Novartis, Unilever, and Infosys. She is based in Chestnut Hill, Massachusetts.

Ellen V. Futter is president of the American Museum of Natural History, one of the world's preeminent scientific, educational, and cultural institutions, with two hundred scientists, one of the world's most important natural history collections, cutting-edge research laboratories, and a tradition of global fieldwork. During her tenure, the museum has been in one of the most active periods of growth in its history. In 2006, it established the Richard Gilder Graduate School and became the first American museum authorized to grant the PhD degree, and it is currently launching the nation's first freestanding museum-based Master of Arts in Teaching program, focused on Earth science. Futter served as a commissioner on the Carnegie-IAS Commission on Mathematics and Science Education. Previously, she served as president of Barnard College for thirteen years. She began her career practicing law at Milbank, Tweed, Hadley & McCloy. Futter serves on the boards of the Brookings Institution, Memorial Sloan-Kettering Cancer Center, JPMorgan Chase, and Consolidated Edison and was previously chairman of the board of the Federal Reserve Bank of New York. She is a fellow of the American Academy of Arts and Sciences and a member of the Council on Foreign Relations and the American Philosophical Society.

Preston M. Geren is president of the Sid W. Richardson Foundation, which provides grants to educational, health, human service, and cultural nonprofit organizations in Texas. He assumed the position in July 2011, after serving as senior adviser and president-elect of the foundation since March 2010. Prior to joining the foundation, Geren served in the Department of Defense from 2001 to 2009 as special assistant to the secretary of defense, acting secretary of the Air Force, undersecretary of the Army, and secretary of the Army. He served four terms as a U.S. congressman in the twelfth district of Texas (1989–97), and was formerly assistant to U.S. senator Lloyd Bentsen. Geren is a director of Anadarko Petroleum Corp. A lawyer and former business executive, he has held leadership positions in numerous civic, educational, business, and philanthropic organizations in Texas. He earned his BA in history at the University of Texas (UT) at Austin and his JD at UT Law School. He studied architecture at Georgia Tech before transferring to UT. A Fort Worth native, he is married and has three daughters.

Louis V. Gerstner Jr. was chairman of the board and chief executive officer of IBM Corporation from 1993 to 2002. Prior to IBM, Gerstner served as chairman and chief executive officer of RJR Nabisco; president of American Express; and a director at McKinsey & Co. He holds a bachelor's degree in engineering from Dartmouth, an MBA from Harvard Business School, and honorary doctorates from a number of U.S. universities. In addition to the Council on Foreign Relations, he is a member of the National Academy of Engineering, a fellow of the American Academy of Arts and Sciences, a director of the Broad Institute of MIT and Harvard, vice chairman of the Memorial Sloan-Kettering Cancer Center, and vice chairman of the American Museum of Natural History. A lifetime advocate of the importance of quality K-12 education, Gerstner created the Teaching Commission in 2003; co-chaired Achieve, an organization of U.S. governors and business leaders driving high academic standards for public schools, from 1996 to 2002; and established, at IBM, Reinventing Education, a strategic partnership through which twenty-one states and school districts utilize IBM technology to eliminate barriers to school reform and improve student performance.

Allan E. Goodman is the sixth president and current CEO of the Institute of International Education (IIE), the leading not-for-profit organization in the field of international educational exchange and development training. IIE conducts research on international academic mobility and administers the Fulbright program sponsored by the U.S. Department of State as well as over 250 other corporate, government, and privately sponsored programs. Previously, he was executive dean of the Walsh School of Foreign Service and a professor at Georgetown University. Goodman served as presidential briefing coordinator for the director of Central Intelligence and as special assistant to the director of the National Foreign Assessment Center in the Carter administration. He is a member of the Council on Foreign Relations, a founding member of the World Innovation Summit for Education, copresident of the Partner University Fund grant review committee, and a member of the Thomas R. Pickering foreign affairs fellowship program and the Jefferson scholarship selection panels. Goodman has a BS from North-western University, an MPA from the John F. Kennedy School of Government, and a PhD in government from Harvard.

Frederick M. Hess is resident scholar and director of education policy studies at the American Enterprise Institute. He has authored several influential books on education, including *The Same Thing Over and Over, Education Unbound, Common Sense School Reform, Revolution at the Margins,* and *Spinning Wheels,* and he pens the *Education Week* blog Rick Hess Straight Up. His work has appeared in scholarly and popular outlets such as the *Teachers College Record, Harvard Education Review, Social Science Quarterly, Urban Affairs Review, American Politics Quarterly, Chronicle of*

Higher Education, Phi Delta Kappan, Educational Leadership, U.S. News & World Report, Washington Post, New York Times, and *National Review.* He has edited widely cited volumes on education philanthropy, stretching the education dollar, the impact of education research, education entrepreneurship, and No Child Left Behind. He serves as executive editor of *Education Next*; as lead faculty member for the Rice Education Entrepreneurship Program; on the review board for the Broad Prize in Urban Education; and on the boards of directors of the National Association of Charter School Authorizers, 4.0 Schools, and the American Board for the Certification of Teaching Excellence. A former high school social studies teacher, he has taught at the University of Virginia, the University of Pennsylvania, Georgetown University, Rice University, and Harvard University. He holds an MA and a PhD in government and an MEd in teaching and curriculum from Harvard University.

Shirley Ann Jackson has been president of Rensselaer Polytechnic Institute (RPI) since 1999 and has held senior leadership positions in government, industry, research, and academe. A theoretical physicist, she was chairman of the U.S. Nuclear Regulatory Commission from 1995 to 1999. She serves on the President's Council of Advisers on Science and Technology, the international security advisory board to the U.S. secretary of state and undersecretary of state for arms control and international security, and the National Commission for Review of Research and Development Programs of the U.S. Intelligence Community. Under her leadership of RPI, new faculty members have been hired, research awards have doubled, and scholarships have increased, and more than $715 million has been invested in new construction, renovations, new equipment, technology, and infrastructure. Jackson is a member of the National Academy of Engineering and the American Philosophical Society and is a fellow of the American Academy of Arts and Sciences, the American Physical Society, and the American Association for the Advancement of Science, of which she is also former president and chairman of the board. She is a regent of the Smithsonian Institution, a member of the boards of the Council on Foreign Relations, the Brookings Institution, IBM, and FedEx, and a vice chair of the Council on Competitiveness, for which she also co-chaired its energy security, innovation, and sustainability initiative. Jackson holds an SB in physics and a PhD in theoretical elementary particle physics, both from MIT.

Joel I. Klein is CEO of the education division and executive vice president in the office of the chairman at News Corporation, where he also serves on the board of directors. Klein was chancellor of the New York City Department of Education, where he oversaw a system of over 1,600 schools with 1.1 million students, 136,000 employees, and a $22 billion budget. In 2002, he launched Children First, a comprehensive reform strategy that has brought coherence and capacity to the system and resulted in significant increases in student performance. He is a former chairman and CEO of Bertelsmann, Inc., a media company. Until September 2000, he served as assistant U.S. attorney general in charge of the antitrust division of the U.S. Department of Justice, and before that he was deputy White House counsel to President Clinton from 1993 to 1995. Klein entered the Clinton administration after twenty years of public and private legal work in Washington, DC. Klein received his BA from Columbia University, earned his JD from Harvard Law School, and has received honorary degrees from Amherst College, Columbia University, Dartmouth College, Duke University, Fordham Law School, Georgetown Law Center, Macaulay Honors College at CUNY, Manhattanville College, New York Law School, and St. John's School of Education. He is the recipient of the NYU Lewis Rudin Award and the Manhattan Institute Alexander Hamilton Award and was recognized as one of *Time* magazine's "Ten People Who Mattered in 1999" and one of "America's 20 Best Leaders in 2006" by *U.S. News & World Report.*

Wendy Kopp is the founder and CEO of Teach For America (TFA), which is building the movement to eliminate educational inequity in the United States by enlisting the nation's most promising future leaders. She is also CEO and cofounder of Teach For All, a global network working to accelerate and increase the impact of this model around the world. Kopp proposed the creation of TFA in her undergraduate senior thesis in 1989. Today more than nine thousand corps members are in the midst of two-year teaching commitments in forty-three regions across the country, reaching over six hundred thousand students, and nearly twenty-four thousand alumni are working inside and outside the field of education to continue the effort to ensure educational excellence and equity. Since 2007, Kopp has led the development of Teach For All to be responsive to requests for support from social entrepreneurs around the world who are passionate about adapting the model. Today, the

Teach For All network includes organizations in twenty-two countries in Europe, Asia, the Americas, and the Middle East, with programs in an additional twenty countries expected to join in the next three years. Kopp is the author of *A Chance to Make History: What Works and What Doesn't in Providing an Excellent Education for All* and *One Day, All Children: The Unlikely Triumph of Teach For America and What I Learned Along the Way*.

Jeffrey T. Leeds is president and cofounder of Leeds Equity Partners, the New York–based private equity firm focused on investments in the knowledge industries. Prior to cofounding Leeds Equity, Leeds specialized in mergers, acquisitions, and corporate finance at Lazard Frères & Co. Prior to joining Lazard, Leeds served as a law clerk to the Honorable William J. Brennan Jr. of the U.S. Supreme Court during the 1985 October term. Leeds was an original trustee of the United Federation of Teachers (UFT) Charter School, the first union-founded charter school in the United States, and was chairman of the board of the Green Dot New York Charter School, located in the Bronx. Leeds currently serves as a director of BarBri, Inc., Education Management Corporation, Instituo de Banca y Comercio, RealPage, Inc. and SeatonCorp. He also serves as a member of the board of directors of the Association of Private Sector Colleges and Universities. He has previously served as a director of Argosy University, Datamark, Miller Heiman, and Ross University, among others.

Julia Levy is the cofounder of Culture Craver, the first social recommendation engine for arts and entertainment, which generates custom recommendations based on the tastes of users' trusted friends and critics. She is also on the associate board of City Year New York, a nonprofit that supports students and teachers in high-needs public schools. Previously, Levy was the director of communications for the New York City Department of Education, where she helped to implement Mayor Michael Bloomberg and Chancellor Joel Klein's Children First school reforms. Earlier in her career, Levy was a reporter, covering education, public policy, and business for publications including the *New York Sun*, the *Financial Times*, and Hearst Newspapers. Levy graduated with an AB from Dartmouth College and an MBA from Columbia Business School.

Michael L. Lomax has been president and CEO of UNCF, the nation's largest private provider of scholarships and other educational support to minority and low-income students, since 2004. Previously, Lomax was president of Dillard University, a literature professor at Morehouse and Spelman colleges, and chairman of the Fulton County Commission in Atlanta, the first African American elected to that post. Throughout his career, Lomax has worked to provide educational opportunities for underrepresented Americans. At UNCF, he oversees its four hundred scholarship programs, including the UNCF Gates Millennium Scholars Program, a twenty-year, $1.6 billion program whose fourteen thousand low-income minority recipients have a 90 percent college graduation rate. He also launched the UNCF Institute for Capacity Building, which helps UNCF's members—thirty-nine historically black colleges and universities—become stronger, more effective, and more self-sustaining. Lomax co-chairs the Education Equality Project and is a member of the Aspen Institute's Commission on No Child Left Behind and the governing boards of Teach For America, the KIPP Foundation, and the National Alliance of Public Charter Schools. He is a frequent contributor to the *National Journal*'s Education Experts blog and author of the MorehouseMan blog at Essence.com. Lomax serves on the boards of the Smithsonian Institution's Museum of African American History and Culture and the Studio Museum of Harlem. He founded the National Black Arts Festival.

Eduardo J. Padrón arrived in the United States as a refugee at age fifteen. Since 1995, he has served as president of Miami Dade College, a national model of student achievement and the largest institution of higher education in America, with more than 174,000 students. An economist by training, Padrón earned his PhD from the University of Florida. In 2009, *Time* magazine included him among the 10 Best College Presidents in the United States. In 2010, *Florida Trend* magazine named him Floridian of the Year. In 2011, the *Washington Post* named him one of the eight most influential college presidents in the United States, and the Carnegie Corporation of New York granted him the prestigious Academic Leadership Award. He is a past board chair of the Association of American Colleges and Universities and the current board chair of the American Council on Education. He has been selected to serve on posts of national prominence by six American presidents. Most recently, President Obama named him chairman of the White House Commission on Educational Excellence for Hispanic Americans. Padrón serves on the boards of the Business/Higher Education Forum, the League for Innovation, RC-2020, the College Board Advocacy and Policy Center, the White House Fellows selection panel, the International Association of University Presidents, and the Council on Foreign Relations.

Matthew F. Pottinger is a combat veteran of the wars in Iraq and Afghanistan. After finishing active duty in the U.S. Marine Corps in 2010, he served as the Edward R. Murrow press fellow at the Council on Foreign Relations. Prior to his military service, Pottinger covered China for the *Wall Street Journal* for several years. He is chief executive officer of China Six LLC, an advisory firm that provides clients with research on Chinese companies.

Laurene Powell Jobs is founder and chair of Emerson Collective, an organization focused on harnessing the potential of individuals from underserved communities to help them build a better life. The collective supports social entrepreneurs and organizations working in the areas of education, social justice, and conservation. It primarily advocates on behalf of underserved students. Powell Jobs also serves as president of the board of College Track, an after-school program she founded in 1997 to prepare underserved high school students for success in college. Started in East Palo Alto, College Track has expanded to serve students in Oakland, San Francisco, New Orleans, and Aurora, Colorado. The program's intensive academic and extracurricular program is designed to ensure admittance to and graduation from college. All of the program's graduates have completed their secondary education and gone on to college. In addition, she serves on the boards of directors of NewSchools Venture Fund, New America Foundation, and Conservation International. She is a member of the Council on Foreign Relations. Powell Jobs holds a BA and a BSE from the University of Pennsylvania and an MBA from the Stanford Graduate School of Business. Earlier in her career, she spent several years working in investment banking and later cofounded a natural foods company in California.

Condoleezza Rice is a professor of political economy in the Graduate School of Business, the Thomas and Barbara Stephenson senior fellow on public policy at the Hoover Institution, and a professor of

political science at Stanford University. She is also a founding partner
of the Rice Hadley Group. Rice served as the sixty-sixth U.S. secretary of state, the second woman and first African-American woman to
hold the post. Rice also served as President George W. Bush's national
security adviser, the first woman to hold the position. Rice served as
Stanford University's provost from 1993 to 1999 and was the institution's chief budget and academic officer. In 1991, Rice cofounded the
Center for a New Generation (CNG), an innovative, after-school academic enrichment program for students in East Palo Alto and East
Menlo Park, California. Previously, Rice served on President George
H.W. Bush's National Security Council staff as director, senior director
of Soviet and East European affairs, and special assistant to the president for national security affairs. In 1986, while an international affairs
fellow at CFR, Rice also served as special assistant to the director of
the joint chiefs of staff. Rice currently serves on the boards of KiOR,
C3, Makena Capital, the George W. Bush Institute, the Commonwealth
Club, the Aspen Institute, the John F. Kennedy Center for the Performing Arts, and the Boys and Girls Clubs of America. She holds a BA and
PhD from the University of Denver and a master's degree from the University of Notre Dame.

Benno C. Schmidt is chairperson of the board of trustees of the City
University of New York (CUNY); chairman of Avenues: The World
School; and interim president and chief executive officer of the Ewing
Marion Kauffman Foundation. Schmidt is a member of the board of
the Council on Aid to Education, a trustee of the National Humanities
Center, a member of the American Academy of Arts and Sciences, and
former chairman and vice chairman of Edison Schools, Inc. Schmidt was
the twentieth president of Yale University and was nationally renowned
for his defense of freedom of expression and the academic values of liberal education. During his presidency, Yale's endowment grew from $1.7
billion to nearly $3 billion, and the largest building program in Yale's his-
tory was initiated. Schmidt was formerly dean of Columbia University
Law School and Harlan Fiske Stone professor of constitutional law. He
is one of the country's leading scholars of the U.S. Constitution, the
history of the U.S. Supreme Court, the law of freedom of expression,
and the history of race relations in America. Schmidt received both his
undergraduate and law degrees from Yale University and served as law
clerk to Supreme Court chief justice Earl Warren.

Stanley S. Shuman is managing director of Allen & Company LLC, with which he has been associated since 1961. He has served as a director of numerous private and public companies, including the News Corporation Limited. He graduated from Harvard College, Harvard Law School, and Harvard Business School. Shuman is trustee emeritus of Phillips Academy at Andover and honorary trustee of the Dalton School. He is chairman of the advisory council for the Center for New York City Law and serves on Harvard's board of overseers committee on university resources. He also serves as trustee of the Markle Foundation and life trustee of WNET. He was previously a trustee of New York Law School and chairman of the board of visitors of the Institute of Policy Sciences and Public Affairs at Duke University. Shuman served as president of the Wiltwyck School, a large residential treatment center with community-based programs for boys from the inner city. He was chairman of the National Economic Development and Law Center, served for nineteen years on the financial control board for New York City, and was a member of President Clinton's foreign intelligence advisory board.

Leigh Morris Sloane serves as the executive director of the Association of Professional Schools of International Affairs (APSIA), where she manages programs and services for APSIA's seventy member schools and affiliates from around the world. With almost twenty years of experience at the intersection of higher education and international affairs, Sloane previously worked as executive director of the Civic Education Project, developing a pilot program with universities in the Middle East. From 2000 to 2002, she was the assistant director for the Congress and U.S. Foreign Policy program at the Council on Foreign Relations, organizing roundtable discussions for senior congressional staff with leading foreign policy experts. In addition, Sloane worked at Harvard's Kennedy School of Government, initially conducting foreign policy research and later as a program officer to establish the Middle East initiative. Her general interest in education reform emerged in the early 1990s while teaching at Veszprém University in Hungary and then as an administrator at the American University in Bulgaria. Sloane earned a BSFS from Georgetown University's Walsh School of Foreign Service and an MSc from the London School of Economics.

Margaret Spellings is the president and CEO of Margaret Spellings and Company and a leading national expert in public policy. She serves as a senior adviser to the U.S. Chamber of Commerce and as president of the chamber's U.S. Forum for Policy Innovation. She is also a senior adviser to the Boston Consulting Group. Spellings served as the U.S. secretary of education from 2005 to 2009, leading the implementation of the No Child Left Behind Act and convening the Commission on the Future of Higher Education. Spellings also served as White House domestic policy adviser under President George W. Bush from 2001 to 2005. Spellings serves on the boards of several funds in the American Funds family managed by the Capital Research and Management Company. She is a member of the ConnectEDU board of directors, as well as America's Promise Alliance, the Broad Center for the Management of School Systems, and Special Olympics. She is also a member of the Goldman Sachs 10,000 Small Businesses advisory council and the Aspen Institute commission to reform the federal appointments process.

Stephen M. Walt is the Robert and Renée Belfer professor of international affairs at the Harvard Kennedy School of Government, where he served as academic dean from 2002 to 2006. He previously taught at Princeton University and the University of Chicago, where he was deputy dean of social sciences. He is a contributing editor at *Foreign Policy* magazine, coeditor of the series *Cornell Studies in Security Affairs,* and co-chair of the editorial board of the journal *International Security.* He was elected a fellow of the American Academy of Arts and Sciences in May 2005. Walt is the author of numerous articles and books on international relations, security studies, and U.S. foreign policy. His books include *The Origins of Alliances,* which received the 1988 Edgar S. Furniss National Security Book Award, and *Taming American Power: The Global Response to U.S. Primacy,* which was a finalist for the Lionel Gelber Prize and the Arthur Ross Book Award. His most recent book, *The Israel Lobby and U.S. Foreign Policy* (coauthored with John J. Mearsheimer) was a *New York Times* best seller and has been translated into twenty foreign languages. His daily blog at *Foreign Policy* can be found at http://walt.foreignpolicy.com.

Randi Weingarten is president of the 1.5-million-member American Federation of Teachers (AFT), AFL-CIO, which represents teachers; paraprofessionals and school-related personnel; higher education faculty and staff; nurses and other health-care professionals; local, state, and federal employees; and early childhood educators. She was elected in July 2008. Weingarten is a reform-minded leader committed to improving schools, hospitals, and public institutions for children, families, and their communities. She has fought to make sure educators are treated with respect and dignity, have a voice in the education of their students, and are given the support and resources they need to succeed in the classroom. In September 2008, Weingarten led the development of the AFT Innovation Fund, a groundbreaking initiative to support sustainable, innovative, and collaborative education projects developed by members and their local unions. In January 2010, the AFT developed a teacher development and evaluation system for schools to determine teachers' problem areas, provide targeted and continuous help, and make fair and expedited employment decisions. From 1996 to 2008, Weingarten was president of the United Federation of Teachers, representing approximately two hundred thousand nonsupervisory New York City public educators and other workers. Weingarten holds degrees from Cornell University's School of Industrial and Labor Relations and the Cardozo School of Law.

Task Force Observers

Observers participate in the Task Force discussions, but are not asked to join the consensus. They participate in their individual, not institutional, capacities.

Edward Alden is the Bernard L. Schwartz senior fellow at the Council on Foreign Relations, specializing in U.S. economic competitiveness. The former Washington bureau chief for the *Financial Times*, his work focuses on immigration and visa policy and on U.S. trade and international economic policy. He codirected the CFR-sponsored Independent Task Force on U.S. Trade and Investment Policy, which was chaired by former White House chief of staff Andrew H. Card and former Senate majority leader Thomas A. Daschle, and was project director for the Independent Task Force on U.S. Immigration Policy. He is the author of the book *The Closing of the American Border: Terrorism, Immigration, and Security Since 9/11*. Alden was previously the Canadian bureau chief for the *Financial Times* based in Toronto and a reporter at the *Vancouver Sun*, specializing in labor and employment issues. He also worked as the managing editor of the newsletter *Inside U.S. Trade*, widely recognized as the leading source of reporting on U.S. trade policies. Alden holds a BA in political science from the University of British Columbia. He holds an MA in international relations from the University of California, Berkeley, and pursued doctoral studies before returning to a journalism career.

Irina A. Faskianos is vice president for the National Program and Outreach at the Council on Foreign Relations. Faskianos directs programming for CFR members residing outside the New York and Washington, DC, areas. She is also responsible for CFR's Outreach initiatives, which target three constituencies—educators and students, religious leaders and scholars, and state and local officials. The objective of the Outreach initiatives is to connect CFR with—and make it a resource on foreign policy for—these groups of interested citizens. Previously, she served as deputy national director and then national director, working to increase the quality and quantity of CFR programming in select cities throughout the United States and abroad. Faskianos was also associate producer of CFR's weekly radio broadcast on NPR and assistant director of media projects. She received a BA cum laude and an MM from Yale University.

David J. Johns is the senior education policy adviser to the Senate Committee on Health, Education, Labor, and Pensions. Prior to working for committee chairman Tom Harkin, Johns had the distinct honor of serving under the leadership of Senator Edward M. Kennedy. Previously, Johns was a Congressional Black Caucus Foundation fellow in the office of Congressman Charles B. Rangel. Johns is the founder of DJJ Consulting, a boutique firm committed to increasing underserved students' access to and quality of educational opportunities. Johns is a member of the Magic Johnson Taylor Michaels Scholarship Program committee and director of development for IMPACT, an organization founded to increase knowledge in the political and legislative process and to enhance economic empowerment opportunities for young professionals. Johns is also on the board of Plan for Success. He is also an adjunct professorial lecturer at American University, currently teaching a graduate-level course on education and the American political system. Johns graduated from Columbia University in 2004 with a triple major in English, creative writing, and African-American studies. His research as an Andrew W. Mellon fellow served as a catalyst to identify, disrupt, and supplant deleterious perceptions of black males within academia and society. Johns obtained a master's degree in sociology and education policy at Columbia while teaching elementary school in New York City.

Kay King is president of King Strategies, an international relations consulting practice that advises clients on long-range planning, strategic communications, program management, and project development. Previously, she served as a vice president at the Council on Foreign Relations (CFR), where she led the Washington office, ran special projects, and authored a study on Congress and national security. Earlier in her career, King held several positions on CFR's staff in New York, including as associate director of the European-American relations project and as editorial assistant at *Foreign Affairs*. Prior to returning to CFR in 2007, King worked extensively in the nonprofit arena in Washington, DC. She was vice president for external relations at the Center for Strategic and International Studies; director of congressional and public affairs at the U.S. Institute of Peace; and the first executive director of the Association of Professional Schools of International Affairs for nearly a decade. King has also served in both the executive and legislative branches of government. She was a deputy assistant secretary of state for legislative affairs in the Clinton administration and was senior legislative assistant for foreign and defense policy to then senator Joseph R. Biden Jr. King holds a bachelor's degree in political science from Vassar College and a master's degree from Columbia University's School of International and Public Affairs.

Kimberly McClure is a Foreign Service officer with the U.S. Department of State and currently serves as deputy director of the 100,000 Strong initiative, an Obama administration initiative launched in May 2010 that seeks to increase the number of American students studying in China. Following assignments to India and Afghanistan, McClure worked as special assistant to Ambassador Richard Holbrooke, the U.S. special representative for Afghanistan and Pakistan; completed an international affairs fellowship with the Council on Foreign Relations; and worked in the U.S. State Department's Bureau of Human Resources and Operations Center. McClure holds a BA in international relations from Stanford University and an MPP from Harvard University's Kennedy School. She has lived in Brazil, Egypt, India, and Afghanistan, and she speaks Portuguese, Spanish, and Dari. She is involved in several projects exploring the nexus between U.S. global competitiveness, education, and national security. She has helped develop two initiatives: the Global Gateways Summer Institute, developed with Global Kids, Inc., which introduces underserved high school students to global issues and international careers; and the Global Access Pipeline, a consortium of nonprofits, universities, and research/policy institutions working to increase diversity in the field of international affairs.

Independent Task Force Reports

Published by the Council on Foreign Relations

U.S. Trade and Investment Policy
Andrew H. Card and Thomas A. Daschle, Chairs; Edward Alden and Matthew J. Slaughter, Project Directors
Independent Task Force Report No. 67 (2011)

Global Brazil and U.S.-Brazil Relations
Samuel W. Bodman and James D. Wolfensohn, Chairs; Julia E. Sweig, Project Director
Independent Task Force Report No. 66 (2011)

U.S. Strategy for Pakistan and Afghanistan
Richard L. Armitage and Samuel R. Berger, Chairs; Daniel S. Markey, Project Director
Independent Task Force Report No. 65 (2010)

U.S. Policy Toward the Korean Peninsula
Charles L. Pritchard and John H. Tilelli Jr., Chairs; Scott A. Snyder, Project Director
Independent Task Force Report No. 64 (2010)

U.S. Immigration Policy
Jeb Bush and Thomas F. McLarty III, Chairs; Edward Alden, Project Director
Independent Task Force Report No. 63 (2009)

U.S. Nuclear Weapons Policy
William J. Perry and Brent Scowcroft, Chairs; Charles D. Ferguson, Project Director
Independent Task Force Report No. 62 (2009)

Confronting Climate Change: A Strategy for U.S. Foreign Policy
George E. Pataki and Thomas J. Vilsack, Chairs; Michael A. Levi, Project Director
Independent Task Force Report No. 61 (2008)

U.S.-Latin America Relations: A New Direction for a New Reality
Charlene Barshefsky and James T. Hill, Chairs; Shannon O'Neil, Project Director
Independent Task Force Report No. 60 (2008)

U.S.-China Relations: An Affirmative Agenda, A Responsible Course
Carla A. Hills and Dennis C. Blair, Chairs; Frank Sampson Jannuzi, Project Director
Independent Task Force Report No. 59 (2007)

National Security Consequences of U.S. Oil Dependency
John Deutch and James R. Schlesinger, Chairs; David G. Victor, Project Director
Independent Task Force Report No. 58 (2006)

Russia's Wrong Direction: What the United States Can and Should Do
John Edwards and Jack Kemp, Chairs; Stephen Sestanovich, Project Director
Independent Task Force Report No. 57 (2006)

More than Humanitarianism: A Strategic U.S. Approach Toward Africa
Anthony Lake and Christine Todd Whitman, Chairs; Princeton N. Lyman and J. Stephen
Morrison, Project Directors
Independent Task Force Report No. 56 (2006)

In the Wake of War: Improving Post-Conflict Capabilities
Samuel R. Berger and Brent Scowcroft, Chairs; William L. Nash, Project Director; Mona K.
Sutphen, Deputy Director
Independent Task Force Report No. 55 (2005)

In Support of Arab Democracy: Why and How
Madeleine K. Albright and Vin Weber, Chairs; Steven A. Cook, Project Director
Independent Task Force Report No. 54 (2005)

Building a North American Community
John P. Manley, Pedro Aspe, and William F. Weld, Chairs; Thomas d'Aquino, Andrés
Rozental, and Robert Pastor, Vice Chairs; Chappell H. Lawson, Project Director
Independent Task Force Report No. 53 (2005)

Iran: Time for a New Approach
Zbigniew Brzezinski and Robert M. Gates, Chairs; Suzanne Maloney, Project Director
Independent Task Force Report No. 52 (2004)

An Update on the Global Campaign Against Terrorist Financing
Maurice R. Greenberg, Chair; William F. Wechsler and Lee S. Wolosky, Project Directors
Independent Task Force Report No. 40B (Web-only release, 2004)

Renewing the Atlantic Partnership
Henry A. Kissinger and Lawrence H. Summers, Chairs; Charles A. Kupchan, Project Director
Independent Task Force Report No. 51 (2004)

Iraq: One Year After
Thomas R. Pickering and James R. Schlesinger, Chairs; Eric P. Schwartz, Project Consultant
Independent Task Force Report No. 43C (Web-only release, 2004)

Nonlethal Weapons and Capabilities
Paul X. Kelley and Graham Allison, Chairs; Richard L. Garwin, Project Director
Independent Task Force Report No. 50 (2004)

*New Priorities in South Asia: U.S. Policy Toward India, Pakistan, and Afghanistan
(Chairmen's Report)*
Marshall Bouton, Nicholas Platt, and Frank G. Wisner, Chairs; Dennis Kux and Mahnaz
Ispahani, Project Directors
Independent Task Force Report No. 49 (2003)
Cosponsored with the Asia Society

Finding America's Voice: A Strategy for Reinvigorating U.S. Public Diplomacy
Peter G. Peterson, Chair; Kathy Bloomgarden, Henry Grunwald, David E. Morey, and

Shibley Telhami, Working Committee Chairs; Jennifer Sieg, Project Director; Sharon Herbstman, Project Coordinator
Independent Task Force Report No. 48 (2003)

Emergency Responders: Drastically Underfunded, Dangerously Unprepared
Warren B. Rudman, Chair; Richard A. Clarke, Senior Adviser; Jamie F. Metzl, Project Director
Independent Task Force Report No. 47 (2003)

Iraq: The Day After (Chairs' Update)
Thomas R. Pickering and James R. Schlesinger, Chairs; Eric P. Schwartz, Project Director
Independent Task Force Report No. 43B (Web-only release, 2003)

Burma: Time for Change
Mathea Falco, Chair
Independent Task Force Report No. 46 (2003)

Afghanistan: Are We Losing the Peace?
Marshall Bouton, Nicholas Platt, and Frank G. Wisner, Chairs; Dennis Kux and Mahnaz Ispahani, Project Directors
Chairman's Report of an Independent Task Force (2003)
Cosponsored with the Asia Society

Meeting the North Korean Nuclear Challenge
Morton I. Abramowitz and James T. Laney, Chairs; Eric Heginbotham, Project Director
Independent Task Force Report No. 45 (2003)

Chinese Military Power
Harold Brown, Chair; Joseph W. Prueher, Vice Chair; Adam Segal, Project Director
Independent Task Force Report No. 44 (2003)

Iraq: The Day After
Thomas R. Pickering and James R. Schlesinger, Chairs; Eric P. Schwartz, Project Director
Independent Task Force Report No. 43 (2003)

Threats to Democracy: Prevention and Response
Madeleine K. Albright and Bronislaw Geremek, Chairs; Morton H. Halperin, Director; Elizabeth Frawley Bagley, Associate Director
Independent Task Force Report No. 42 (2002)

America—Still Unprepared, Still in Danger
Gary Hart and Warren B. Rudman, Chairs; Stephen E. Flynn, Project Director
Independent Task Force Report No. 41 (2002)

Terrorist Financing
Maurice R. Greenberg, Chair; William F. Wechsler and Lee S. Wolosky, Project Directors
Independent Task Force Report No. 40 (2002)

Enhancing U.S. Leadership at the United Nations
David Dreier and Lee H. Hamilton, Chairs; Lee Feinstein and Adrian Karatnycky, Project Directors
Independent Task Force Report No. 39 (2002)
Cosponsored with Freedom House

Improving the U.S. Public Diplomacy Campaign in the War Against Terrorism
Carla A. Hills and Richard C. Holbrooke, Chairs; Charles G. Boyd, Project Director
Independent Task Force Report No. 38 (Web-only release, 2001)

Building Support for More Open Trade
Kenneth M. Duberstein and Robert E. Rubin, Chairs; Timothy F. Geithner, Project Director;
Daniel R. Lucich, Deputy Project Director
Independent Task Force Report No. 37 (2001)

Beginning the Journey: China, the United States, and the WTO
Robert D. Hormats, Chair; Elizabeth Economy and Kevin Nealer, Project Directors
Independent Task Force Report No. 36 (2001)

Strategic Energy Policy Update
Edward L. Morse, Chair; Amy Myers Jaffe, Project Director
Independent Task Force Report No. 33B (2001)
Cosponsored with the James A. Baker III Institute for Public Policy of Rice University

Testing North Korea: The Next Stage in U.S. and ROK Policy
Morton I. Abramowitz and James T. Laney, Chairs; Robert A. Manning, Project Director
Independent Task Force Report No. 35 (2001)

The United States and Southeast Asia: A Policy Agenda for the New Administration
J. Robert Kerrey, Chair; Robert A. Manning, Project Director
Independent Task Force Report No. 34 (2001)

Strategic Energy Policy: Challenges for the 21st Century
Edward L. Morse, Chair; Amy Myers Jaffe, Project Director
Independent Task Force Report No. 33 (2001)
Cosponsored with the James A. Baker III Institute for Public Policy of Rice University

A Letter to the President and a Memorandum on U.S. Policy Toward Brazil
Stephen Robert, Chair; Kenneth Maxwell, Project Director
Independent Task Force Report No. 32 (2001)

State Department Reform
Frank C. Carlucci, Chair; Ian J. Brzezinski, Project Coordinator
Independent Task Force Report No. 31 (2001)
Cosponsored with the Center for Strategic and International Studies

U.S.-Cuban Relations in the 21st Century: A Follow-on Report
Bernard W. Aronson and William D. Rogers, Chairs; Julia Sweig and Walter Mead, Project
Directors
Independent Task Force Report No. 30 (2000)

Toward Greater Peace and Security in Colombia: Forging a Constructive U.S. Policy
Bob Graham and Brent Scowcroft, Chairs; Michael Shifter, Project Director
Independent Task Force Report No. 29 (2000)
Cosponsored with the Inter-American Dialogue

Future Directions for U.S. Economic Policy Toward Japan
Laura D'Andrea Tyson, Chair; M. Diana Helweg Newton, Project Director
Independent Task Force Report No. 28 (2000)

First Steps Toward a Constructive U.S. Policy in Colombia
Bob Graham and Brent Scowcroft, Chairs; Michael Shifter, Project Director
Interim Report (2000)
Cosponsored with the Inter-American Dialogue

Promoting Sustainable Economies in the Balkans
Steven Rattner, Chair; Michael B.G. Froman, Project Director
Independent Task Force Report No. 27 (2000)

Non-Lethal Technologies: Progress and Prospects
Richard L. Garwin, Chair; W. Montague Winfield, Project Director
Independent Task Force Report No. 26 (1999)

Safeguarding Prosperity in a Global Financial System:
The Future International Financial Architecture
Carla A. Hills and Peter G. Peterson, Chairs; Morris Goldstein, Project Director
Independent Task Force Report No. 25 (1999)
Cosponsored with the International Institute for Economics

U.S. Policy Toward North Korea: Next Steps
Morton I. Abramowitz and James T. Laney, Chairs; Michael J. Green, Project Director
Independent Task Force Report No. 24 (1999)

Reconstructing the Balkans
Morton I. Abramowitz and Albert Fishlow, Chairs; Charles A. Kupchan, Project Director
Independent Task Force Report No. 23 (Web-only release, 1999)

Strengthening Palestinian Public Institutions
Michel Rocard, Chair; Henry Siegman, Project Director; Yezid Sayigh and Khalil Shikaki,
Principal Authors
Independent Task Force Report No. 22 (1999)

U.S. Policy Toward Northeastern Europe
Zbigniew Brzezinski, Chair; F. Stephen Larrabee, Project Director
Independent Task Force Report No. 21 (1999)

The Future of Transatlantic Relations
Robert D. Blackwill, Chair and Project Director
Independent Task Force Report No. 20 (1999)

U.S.-Cuban Relations in the 21st Century
Bernard W. Aronson and William D. Rogers, Chairs; Walter Russell Mead, Project Director
Independent Task Force Report No. 19 (1999)

After the Tests: U.S. Policy Toward India and Pakistan
Richard N. Haass and Morton H. Halperin, Chairs
Independent Task Force Report No. 18 (1998)
Cosponsored with the Brookings Institution

Managing Change on the Korean Peninsula
Morton I. Abramowitz and James T. Laney, Chairs; Michael J. Green, Project Director
Independent Task Force Report No. 17 (1998)

Promoting U.S. Economic Relations with Africa
Peggy Dulany and Frank Savage, Chairs; Salih Booker, Project Director
Independent Task Force Report No. 16 (1998)

U.S. Middle East Policy and the Peace Process
Henry Siegman, Project Coordinator
Independent Task Force Report No. 15 (1997)

Differentiated Containment: U.S. Policy Toward Iran and Iraq
Zbigniew Brzezinski and Brent Scowcroft, Chairs; Richard W. Murphy, Project Director
Independent Task Force Report No. 14 (1997)

Russia, Its Neighbors, and an Enlarging NATO
Richard G. Lugar, Chair; Victoria Nuland, Project Director
Independent Task Force Report No. 13 (1997)

Rethinking International Drug Control: New Directions for U.S. Policy
Mathea Falco, Chair
Independent Task Force Report No. 12 (1997)

Financing America's Leadership: Protecting American Interests and Promoting American Values
Mickey Edwards and Stephen J. Solarz, Chairs; Morton H. Halperin, Lawrence J. Korb,
and Richard M. Moose, Project Directors
Independent Task Force Report No. 11 (1997)
Cosponsored with the Brookings Institution

A New U.S. Policy Toward India and Pakistan
Richard N. Haass, Chair; Gideon Rose, Project Director
Independent Task Force Report No. 10 (1997)

Arms Control and the U.S.-Russian Relationship
Robert D. Blackwill, Chair and Author; Keith W. Dayton, Project Director
Independent Task Force Report No. 9 (1996)
Cosponsored with the Nixon Center for Peace and Freedom

American National Interest and the United Nations
George Soros, Chair
Independent Task Force Report No. 8 (1996)

Making Intelligence Smarter: The Future of U.S. Intelligence
Maurice R. Greenberg, Chair; Richard N. Haass, Project Director
Independent Task Force Report No. 7 (1996)

Lessons of the Mexican Peso Crisis
John C. Whitehead, Chair; Marie-Josée Kravis, Project Director
Independent Task Force Report No. 6 (1996)

Managing the Taiwan Issue: Key Is Better U.S. Relations with China
Stephen Friedman, Chair; Elizabeth Economy, Project Director
Independent Task Force Report No. 5 (1995)

Non-Lethal Technologies: Military Options and Implications
Malcolm H. Wiener, Chair
Independent Task Force Report No. 4 (1995)

Should NATO Expand?
Harold Brown, Chair; Charles A. Kupchan, Project Director
Independent Task Force Report No. 3 (1995)

Success or Sellout? The U.S.-North Korean Nuclear Accord
Kyung Won Kim and Nicholas Platt, Chairs; Richard N. Haass, Project Director
Independent Task Force Report No. 2 (1995)
Cosponsored with the Seoul Forum for International Affairs

Nuclear Proliferation: Confronting the New Challenges
Stephen J. Hadley, Chair; Mitchell B. Reiss, Project Director
Independent Task Force Report No. 1 (1995)

Note: Task Force reports are available for download from CFR's website, www.cfr.org.
For more information, email publications@cfr.org.

CPSIA information can be obtained at www.ICGtesting.com
Printed in the USA
LVOW090015040512

280273LV00005B/2/P